D0519903

Women'sHealth

TAKE IT
ALL OFF!

Keep It
All Off!

Women's Health

TAKE IT ALL OFF!

Keep It All Off!

Women's Health readers reveal
**HOW THEY LOST 20, 50,
EVEN 100 POUNDS—**
and how you can too!

LESLEY ROTCHFORD

HEARST

This book is intended as a reference volume only, not as a medical manual. The information given here is designed to help you make informed decisions about your health. It is not intended as a substitute for any treatment that may have been prescribed by your doctor. If you suspect that you have a medical problem, we urge you to seek competent medical help.

The information in this book is meant to supplement, not replace, proper exercise training. All forms of exercise pose some inherent risks. The editors and publisher advise readers to take full responsibility for their safety and know their limits. Before practicing the exercises in this book, be sure that your equipment is well-maintained, and do not take risks beyond your level of experience, aptitude, training, and fitness. The exercise and dietary programs in this book are not intended as a substitute for any exercise routine or dietary regimen that may have been prescribed by your doctor. As with all exercise and dietary programs, you should get your doctor's approval before beginning.

Mention of specific companies, organizations, or authorities in this book does not imply endorsement by the author or publisher, nor does mention of specific companies, organizations, or authorities imply that they endorse this book, its author, or the publisher.

Internet addresses and phone numbers given in this book were accurate at the time it went to press.

© 2018 by Hearst Inc.

All rights reserved. No part of this publication may be reproduced or transmitted in any form or by any means, electronic or mechanical, including photocopying, recording, or any other information storage and retrieval system, without the written permission of the publisher.

Printed in the United States of America

Photograph credits appear on page 235.

Book design by Christina Gaugler

Library of Congress Cataloging-in-Publication Data is on file with the publisher.

ISBN 978-1-62336-903-3

2 4 6 8 10 9 7 5 3 1

HEARST

For Gil, who proposed to me at the end of the Boston Marathon
12 years ago and has been cheering me on ever since.

CONTENTS

Acknowledgments

I could not have written this book without the brilliant Cassandra Forsythe, PhD, RD, assistant professor of physical education and exercise science at Central Connecticut State University, who created the diet and workout. Thank you for your guidance, patience, and kindness. And, of course, there would be no book without the dozens of weight loss superstars who inspired it.

Thank you to the fitness and nutrition experts who have generously shared their time and tips with me over the years, including Shawn Talbott, to whom I owe my working knowledge of cortisol; Stephen Gullo, who introduced me to GG Bran Crispbread and many other weight loss foods; Jean Kristeller, who taught me the magic of mindful eating; and Nicholas Ratamess, who has good-naturedly fielded my questions about strength training, fat-blasting hormones, and HIIT.

To my friends and former colleagues at *Women's Health*, especially Amy Keller Laird, Theresa O'Rourke, Sara Culley, Jen Ator, Sascha de Gersdorff, and Sarah Rozen, thank you for keeping me part of the *WH* family. And to my editor Erica Sanders-Foege, Leah Polakoff, and the rest of the Hearst team, I am profoundly grateful.

I thank my mentors and former bosses Kate White and Michele Promaulayko.

To my extraordinary parents, Joel and Karen Goober, for believing in me—always. And to my brother, Greg, a true hero.

Finally, thank you to Gil, Wyatt, Henry, and Teddy for bringing endless amounts of love and joy to my life.

Introduction

The first time I went on a diet was in college. My daily runs turned out to be no match for keg beer and late-night pizza, and I started gaining weight. This was back in the late '90s, when baggy vintage Levi's and boxy Patagonia jackets could keep you in denial—so I didn't realize I was packing on pounds until the summer between sophomore and junior year. A childhood friend and I had jobs scooping ice cream on Martha's Vineyard, and we'd apparently been eating as much ice cream as we'd been serving because when our parents arrived for a visit in August, my friend's mom took one look at our significantly stockier figures and exclaimed, "What happened to you girls?"

It was time to face the music. I didn't starve myself or jump on the latest weight loss trend (which at the time was going fat-free, and we know how effective *that* turned out to be). Instead, I just started eating a little less and figured out how much I needed to exercise to make up for the occasional slice of cake or pizza. This strategy has served me well over the years, helping me stay slim and strong despite a demanding, sit-on-my-butt-all-day desk job and three kids younger than 7.

The women in this book have their own weight loss tales to tell. Some of them have shed over 100 pounds—most have dropped over 50—and kept the weight off. Their newfound health and confidence has set in motion a domino effect of positive change. They're an inspiration to me and to everyone who has ever set out on a weight loss journey, which is why I wanted to write this book. On these pages, you will discover the secrets to their success, plus all the tools you need to lose weight and keep it off. My hope is that the Take It All Off Plan helps you develop a passion for fitness and nutrition and sets you on the path to a happier, healthier life.

The Skinny on Taking It All Off

If you've cracked open this book, you're probably looking to lose some weight. Maybe you've been chubby since you were a kid. Maybe you packed it on during college or couldn't take it off after having your first baby. Maybe you're a fluctuator—thin one year, flabby the next. Sound familiar? And chances are you've tried every trendy diet and every popular exercise program—and here you are.

The Take It All Off Plan isn't like other diets—in fact, it's not a diet at all. It's a lifestyle makeover that provides innovative eating strategies with a meal plan that focuses on protein and portion control, plus a time-saving strength and cardio routine specifically designed to blast fat fast. What's more, this program has been shown to work for women just like you, who have struggled for years—in some cases their entire lives—to lose weight and now regularly rock skinny jeans and crush 10-Ks. Their stories are so inspiring that they were featured in the "You Lose, You Win" column of *Women's Health* magazine.

While I was an executive editor at *Women's Health,* I used to push my other work aside when the "You Lose, You Win" page landed on my desk to be edited. Real women sharing their tales of weight loss triumph? I couldn't get enough! After reading dozens of these over the years, I started noticing the common threads—these women were following similar weight loss strategies. It was as if the answers for permanent weight loss were staring at me on the page. And now, with the help of fitness and nutrition expert Cassandra Forsythe, PhD, RD, I'm able to share them with you.

This book is a guaranteed plan for success. It reveals the tricks that worked for the women profiled in the magazine—you'll be hearing from them on these pages, too. I'll be walking (make that power walking!) you through the Take It All Off Plan in the following chapters. But before we get to all of that, here are some amazing physical and psychological benefits you'll get from following this program.

KILLER CONFIDENCE

Imagine how great it would feel to strip off your cover-up and walk down the beach in your swimsuit without worrying about what you look like from behind. Think about what it would be like to enjoy shopping for clothes. Consider the satisfaction of standing in the front row of your fitness class. Here's the thing: When you work your butt off to shed pounds, you can't help but feel good about yourself—your confidence skyrockets, your mood swings into perma-sunny mode, and all that body shame disappears. "I used to run from cameras, but now I like what I see in photos," says Krystal Sanders, 32, of Spring, Texas, who went from 185 to 130 pounds. "I'm finally at peace with the way I look."

In fact, a review of 36 studies, published in the journal *Appetite,*[1] found that participating in a weight loss program improves self-esteem, body image, and health-related quality of life and decreases feelings of depression. Of course, weight loss doesn't guarantee happiness; there are many factors that contribute to contentment, and losing weight isn't going to solve all of your problems. But many people find that a healthier body leads to a better life. *Women's Health* reader Katie Hug, who suffered from anxiety and depression, is one of those people. "Saying I'm in a better mood now is an understatement," says the Idaho native, who dropped a whopping 137 pounds

LOSE WEIGHT, GAIN ENERGY

When Annie Allen, a nurse from Columbus, Ohio, was tipping the scales at nearly 200 pounds, she was as sluggish as her metabolism. "I'd come home [from work] and fall into bed. I had no energy."

As she inched closer to her current weight of 165 (by ditching soda and fast food, cooking healthy meals, and running and cardio boxing), the spring came back to her step. She'd bang out her 12-hour shifts and still have energy to burn at the gym. These days, she boxes twice a week and runs about 10 races a year.

Annie's story is hardly unusual. Research shows that the heavier you get, the more lethargic you become. Your body wastes energy lugging around extra pounds, and excess weight can disrupt your sleep. About half of people who suffer from sleep apnea, a condition that causes pauses in breathing that jolt you out of deep sleep, are overweight.

Losing flab can increase your stamina and alertness. Researchers at the University of Pennsylvania[2] fed one group of mice their normal chow and another group high-fat chow for 8 weeks. During the 9th week, some of the high-fat eaters were put on a diet. At the end of the study, the high-fat group had gained weight and developed a tendency to nod off during the day. But the high-fat eaters put on the 1-week diet lost weight and were a lot less pooped—indicating that even a modest amount of weight loss can have a huge impact on energy levels.

and was able to ditch her mood meds, which she had taken for 17 years. "Endorphins from exercise help me so much! I still battle anxiety, so I use exercise as an outlet. I feel like I woke up from a bad dream."

A LONGER, HEALTHIER LIFE

While many of us are motivated by aesthetic goals (like fitting back into prepregnancy pants or feeling comfortable donning a bikini), you can't beat the health benefits that come with losing weight. Research shows that slimming down fights off disease and helps you live longer. Take cancer, for example: Fat can mess with hormones, immunity, and factors that regulate cell growth, which can boost your risk of colon, rectal, breast, esophageal, kidney, pancreatic, and other types of cancer. (According to the World Cancer Research Fund International, roughly 20 percent of cancers diagnosed in the United States are related to body fatness, inactivity,

"I Did It!"

KATIE'S STORY: During college, a junk-food-heavy diet and a list of 12 meds for anxiety and depression caused Katie's weight to creep up. "The drugs made me sluggish. I ate everything in sight," says Katie. Three kids later, she weighed 270 pounds.

WAKE-UP CALL: At a checkup in 2012, Katie's doctor delivered some unpleasant news. "She said I was morbidly obese, which was horrible to hear."

NAME: **Katie Hug**

AGE: **34**

HOMETOWN: **Kuna, Idaho**

BEFORE WEIGHT: **270**

AFTER WEIGHT: **133**

SUCCESS SECRETS: Katie's first step was enlisting a psychiatrist to help her taper off the meds. Eliminating the drugs "was like coming out of a zonked-out fog," she says. She starting walking around her block each morning and tracked her calories with an app. "I had no idea I was eating around 5,000 a day. I cut that in half," she says. By swapping pasta and refined grains for chicken, turkey, fish, and veggies, Katie dropped 40 pounds in a year. After upping her walks to 3 miles, she started jogging and got a trainer, who prescribed strength training routines that helped her crack 165 pounds. Katie finished her first half-marathon in September 2014. She whittled her calorie count down to 1,800 a day and focused on adding protein and limiting unhealthy fats, two tenets of the Take It All Off Plan. "I made high-protein pancakes by adding egg whites and cottage cheese and had vinaigrette instead of ranch dressing," she says. By June 2015, she was wearing a size 4—and more importantly, felt loads calmer and happier.

and lousy nutrition, and being overweight can contribute to as many as one out of five cancer-related deaths.) A review of research, published in the journal *Diabetes, Obesity and Metabolism,*[3] found that losing weight lowers the incidence of cancer and reduces levels of circulating cancer biomarkers (red-flag-like molecules in blood or body tissue that indicate abnormalities).

Obesity is clearly linked to type 2 diabetes (almost 90 percent of people with type 2 diabetes are overweight). Here's the scoop: Insulin is a hormone produced in the pancreas that helps cells use glucose (sugar) for energy. Fat blocks insulin from opening cell "doors"—think of it as a deadbolt—so the pancreas pumps out more insulin to help crack those doors open enough to allow glucose to sneak in. But if your pancreas can't keep up with the demand for insulin, glucose collects in the bloodstream, and you can eventually wind up with type 2 diabetes. All of this can be avoided by losing body fat, shows a study in the journal *Diabetes Care.*[4] (Every kilogram—or 2.2 pounds—of weight loss was associated with a 16 percent reduction of diabetes risk.)

Obesity and insulin resistance can also impact your fertility by raising your chances of developing polycystic ovary syndrome (about 40 to 80 percent of women with this disease are overweight). Experts believe that excess insulin causes the body to overproduce male sex hormones called androgens that can prevent ovulation and make it difficult to get pregnant. A study in the *Journal of Clinical Endocrinology & Metabolism*[5] shows that if you suffer from polycystic ovary syndrome, losing weight can improve your chances of getting pregnant and having a baby.

Obesity causes heart disease in a few different ways. Fat increases inflammatory biomarkers, which can damage the walls of your arteries, and it raises "bad" LDL cholesterol and lowers "good" HDL cholesterol, resulting in plaque buildup in your heart vessels. It also restricts blood circulation and forces the heart to work harder, which can cause damage and disease.

The good news is that losing just 5 percent of your weight can reduce your risk of both diabetes and heart disease, found a study in the journal *Cell Metabolism.*[6] Shedding the pounds will also prevent blood clots and stroke by lowering blood pressure. Dutch researchers[7] conducted a review of studies and found that dropping weight—especially more than 11 pounds—had a significant impact on blood pressure.

The Take It All Off Plan can prevent gallstones, too (pebblelike masses that develop in the gallbladder and can be painful). Obesity increases the amount of cholesterol in bile (a fluid produced by the liver to shuttle toxins and waste out of the body), and cholesterol promotes stone formation. But there's a catch: If you starve yourself to lose weight, your liver will respond by dumping extra cholesterol into the bile. Research published in the *International Journal of Obesity*[8] found that a very-low-calorie diet increased the likelihood of stones three times more than a low-calorie diet (1,200 to 1,500 calories per day). The number of calories you eat on this program will vary according to your current weight (more on that in Chapter 7), but the Take It All Off Plan is designed to keep your calories in a range that promotes weight loss without going so low that you put yourself at risk for gallstones.

NO MORE ACHES AND PAINS

Another perk to completing the Take It All Off Plan: Your knees won't kill you anymore. Being overweight affects all of your joints, but no joints take more of a beating than your poor knees. When you walk on level ground, the pressure on your knees is roughly one and a half times your body weight. The force on your knees shoots up to two to three times your body weight when you go up or down an incline (like hills or stairs). Bending down to pick something up is your knees' least favorite task, as that ups the load to five times your body weight. You know that crunching noise your knees sometimes make? That's your joints screaming in agony! (Weight gain can also cause inflammation that can prevent joints from working properly.)

If you add more weight to your frame than your knees are designed to carry, you'll wind up wearing down the joints, a condition referred to as osteoarthritis (if you think you're too young to have to worry about this, you're not; it can happen as early as your twenties). A study in the journal *Arthritis & Rheumatism*[9] of overweight adults with knee

RATE YOUR RISK

Answer the following questions to find out if you're genetically predisposed to any obesity-related conditions. If you end up with a yes (or a few yeses), don't freak—it doesn't mean you're automatically going to get any of this stuff. Just consider it another reason to take control of your health with the Take It All Off Plan.

Have either of your parents or any of your siblings suffered from:

Heart attack or heart surgery before age 55?	Yes/No
Stroke before age 50?	Yes/No
Congenital heart disease?	Yes/No
Hypertension?	Yes/No
Cancer before age 60?	Yes/No
High cholesterol?	Yes/No
Diabetes?	Yes/No
Obesity?	Yes/No

Chart from the ACSM Health Status & Health History Questionnaire UP and Running Integrated Sports Medical Center

osteoarthritis revealed that losing 1 pound of weight took 4 pounds of pressure off the knees. So ditching just 5 pounds would relieve 20 pounds of pressure from your already over-burdened knees. When Anu Sharma, 39, of Mountain House, California, weighed 250 pounds, her knee pain was so severe that she couldn't walk up the stairs to her second floor apartment. She eventually lost 78 pounds by cutting out junk food and doing a combination of running, working out on the elliptical, weight training, and TRX (developed by Navy SEALs!). Today, she feels zero knee pain —and not only can she walk up stairs, she can run up them. Sharma loves it when her 11-year-old daughter mentions—as she does frequently—how strong her mom looks, especially when Anu takes two at a time.

A RED-HOT RELATIONSHIP

Whoever came up with the traditional marriage vows should have slipped in the line "in thinness and in fatness," because losing weight can alter a relationship—often in a good way! Think about it like this: You're changing, so your relationship is going to change, too. When you feel beautiful, strong, and energetic, you have more to bring to your union. And as our happy "losers" discovered, it's especially effective to team up with your partner. Sarah Russello, 34, from Clarks Summit, Pennsylvania, regularly hit the gym

NAME: **Bridget Rauschenberg**
AGE: **32**
HOMETOWN: **Raleigh, North Carolina**
BEFORE WEIGHT: **284**
AFTER WEIGHT: **158**

with her martial arts instructor hubby and ditched 47 pounds. It's a routine she continues today. "It's great motivation. I know he's watching me, so I try harder," she says. For busy people (in other words, all of us),

(continued on page 10)

"I Did It!"

NAME: **Anu Sharma**

AGE: **39**

HOMETOWN: **Mountain House, California**

BEFORE WEIGHT: **250**

AFTER WEIGHT: **172**

ANU'S STORY: Anu became pregnant and interpreted "eating for two" liberally. After having her baby, Anu continued to eat junk to comfort herself. She was unemployed and going through a stressful move. At 5 feet 10 inches, her weight hovered around 250 pounds.

WAKE-UP CALL: One morning in April 2009, as Anu struggled up the stairs to her second-floor apartment, knee pain stopped her short. "It was terrifying that I felt pain when I was only 31," she says. "What was going to happen to me when I was 50?" The very next day, she laced up her dusty workout shoes and joined a gym.

SUCCESS SECRETS: At first, Anu walked on the treadmill or used the elliptical for 20 minutes a day. After 6 months, she was 35 pounds lighter and running an hour, plus doing 30 minutes on the elliptical daily. She shed another 15 pounds after she started avoiding the cookie aisle and making veggie burritos instead of ordering subs.

Later, a personal trainer taught her heavy barbell moves, like deadlifts and overhead squats, as well as plyometrics. "I was amazed by how defined my muscles started to look," she says. "It's led me to teach my daughter to be athletic and strong rather than skinny and weak."

Now, Anu isn't just a gym rat—she's a gym owner, running three Curves locations. "I love showing my clients they can change their lives," she says. She spends her free time prepping meals for herself and her family. "I've had my members ask if I get tired of eating this way, and my answer is, "Are you asking me if I'm tired of feeling this good? My answer is no!" Anu says she never gets sick and credits her good fortune to eating right, exercising, and living a healthy lifestyle. "If you don't take care of yourself, you won't be well enough to rake care of everyone else," she says.

working out together has the huge side benefit of sweat time doubling as couple time. Think about it: You've got more confidence, you're losing weight and looking better than ever—any doubt that will have an effect on your romantic life? We'll look at that more in a sec.

Slimming down can give you the confidence to pursue love, too. That was the case for Jen Kelley, 31, of Warren, Rhode Island, who lost a whopping 91 pounds. "If I hadn't gotten in shape, I wouldn't have started dating online and eventually met my husband," she says.

That includes self-love. The weight loss journey can lead to a stronger sense of acceptance and love for who you are.

Take Bridget Rauschenberg of Raleigh, North Carolina, for example, who broke up with her boyfriend after she gained more than 80 pounds during college. "I was disgusted by how I looked, but I kept saying I'd lose weight later," Bridget says. "One reason we split is because I needed to get my life back on track." A chance encounter with her ex on Valentine's Day, 4 months after their breakup, reminded her that she'd made zero progress and still needed to take control of her life. She cleaned up her diet, started working out, and over time shed 126 pounds. In the end, she realized the relationship was not the reason to get healthy—she was! As for her ex? "I haven't looked back," she says.

Let's Talk about Sex

And about that romance thing: Losing weight the Take It All Off way can boost your confidence in the bedroom. When you're fit and slim, you want to show off your body (keep the lights on, please!), and you're freed up to focus on your own pleasure, as opposed to worrying about the size of your thighs or trying to twist yourself into positions that hide your belly pooch. Research from Duke University Medical Center[10] showed that obese people were 25 percent more likely to be dissatisfied with their sex lives than people of normal weight and that dropping around 12 percent of body weight can help you reclaim your mojo. Just ask Anu Sharma, whose weight loss improved not only her joint pain but her sex life, too: "Things with my husband are seriously spicy now that I'm so much more confident," she says.

SO HOW MANY POUNDS DO I NEED TO DROP?

Plenty of research has shown that BMI (body mass index) is an accurate measurement of body fatness, but the method has its fair share of haters—including scientists who bashed it in an editorial in the journal *Science*.[11] The beef with BMI? Being fit can throw off the numbers. In other words, bone is heavier than muscle and muscle is heavier than fat, so if

"YOU LOSE, YOU WIN" HALL OF FAME

A special shout-out to the women featured in the monthly *Women's Health* "You Lose, You Win" column who lost *100 pounds or more.* Ladies, without you, our dreams would not be as bright.

- Christina Donatella (180 pounds)
- Katie Hug (137 pounds)
- Brandy Thele (130 pounds)
- Bridget Rauschenberg (126 pounds)
- DJ Gray (115 pounds)
- Larissa Reggetto (105 pounds)
- Zakiee Labib (104 pounds)
- Kim Schoenfeldt (103 pounds)
- Donesha Bolden (100 pounds)
- Sarah DeArmond (100 pounds)
- Jessie Foss (100 pounds)
- Brittany Hicks (110 pounds)
- Ashley Nunn (120 pounds)

you exercise to the point of developing strong bones (good) and muscles (also good), you might edge into the overweight category, even though you're perfectly, or even exceptionally, healthy. BMI also doesn't factor in fat distribution. Visceral fat (the kind buried deep within the abdomen) increases health risks more than subcutaneous fat (the pinchable kind that spills over the waist of your pants).

But for the average person, BMI remains the gold standard for gauging fatness. To find your body mass index, divide your weight (in pounds) by your height (in inches) squared, and then multiply that number by 703. (Or save yourself the trouble and use the online BMI calculator at cdc.gov.) If your BMI clocks in below 18.5, you're underweight; if it falls between 18.5 and 24.9, congrats, you're at a healthy weight; if it's between 25 and 29.9, you're overweight; and anything over 30 means you're clinically obese (sorry!). So if you're 5 feet 5 inches and weigh 150 pounds, the equation will look like this: $150 \div 65^2 \times 703$, which equals a healthy-by-a-hair BMI of 24.96. To find out how much you need to lose, start plugging in lower weights until your number falls into the healthy weight category.

Making the Change

Some of the women featured in this book lost over 100 pounds. Think about that, *100 pounds*. Pretty incredible, right? The Take It All Off Plan can help you achieve triple-digit weight loss—or help you lose 20, 10, or even just those lingering last 5 pounds. The key to getting the results you want is to replace unhealthy habits with healthy ones. You may have heard that it takes 21 days to develop a new habit—like working out every morning or eating a salad for lunch. But British researchers[1] say it actually takes a little longer—closer to 66 days. Still, that's a pretty short amount of time, considering this is something you're going to be doing for the rest of your life!

When people give up pursuing a new habit before those 66 days have elapsed, it's often because there was something wrong with the habit, not the person. In other words, you don't want to set a goal for yourself that's nearly impossible to stick to or that's so intense you'll burn out before the behavior becomes second nature. Start off by establishing healthy habits that are specific and manageable. For example, instead of saying "I'm going to go to the gym every morning," vow to go three times a week. Once the habit of working out three times a week has become engrained, you'll want to go to the gym more often because it makes you feel good.

You're probably wondering about ditching bad habits. Okay, that's trickier, as it can be harder to give something up that you have been doing for years than to embark on something new and exciting. Make it easier by focusing on developing a new habit that's related to the one you're trying to kick.

- If you're trying to swear off desserts, make a habit of eating fruit as a snack (you'll automatically end up replacing sugary treats with fruit).

- If you're aiming to give up fast food, make a habit of cooking at home most nights (whipping up homemade meals means you'll have no reason to hit the drive-thru).

- If you want to stop drinking diet soda, make a habit of drinking calorie-free flavored seltzer (the carbonation mimics the soda experience).

- If you want to ditch white carbs, make a habit of eating more whole grains (the whole grains will naturally take the place of junky starches on your plate).

- If you're trying to stop eating in front of the TV, make a habit of playing soothing music while you dine (we often turn on the TV for background noise).

Now that you know how to create a healthy habit (and kick a bad one), here are four key practices to put in place before embarking on your weight loss journey.

STEP #1: TOSS THE TEMPTATIONS

Bags of chips. Tubs of pretzels. Leftover Halloween candy. Make life easier for yourself by tossing anything tempting. It's especially important to ditch your "trigger" foods—those foods that you tend to binge on. I will eat sugary cereal by the handful if it's in my house. Freshly baked chocolate chip cookies defy my willpower. Anything graham-crackery? Forget it.

Take It All Off superstar Brandy Thele, who lost 130 pounds after she was diagnosed with type 2 diabetes, has the same philosophy. "If you know you'll break into the leftover birthday cake at midnight, toss it immediately," she says.

If you can't throw something out—like, say, the chocolates in the office candy jar—practice avoidance. Take a different route to the bathroom so you aren't tempted to pop a piece of candy in your mouth every time you walk by. If your partner or kids will revolt if you chuck the ice cream, hide it behind the frozen edamame so you aren't confronted by it every

NAME: **Brandy Thele**

AGE: **37**

HOMETOWN: **Yukon, Oklahoma**

BEFORE WEIGHT: **275**

AFTER WEIGHT: **145**

A while back I was in a Martha Stewart phase and would place a glass-domed cake plate filled with homemade cookies, cupcakes, or brownies on my kitchen island. Oh boy, bad idea. Whenever I stood there answering e-mails or talking to my kids while they ate dinner, I'd start mindlessly munching on the baked goods. Research from the Cornell University Food and Brand Lab[2] shows that leaving food out is associated with a higher weight. People who left ready-to-eat foods out on the counter weighed an average of 20-plus pounds more than people who put food away immediately. If you want to keep a snack on the counter, opt for produce. The study found that women who left a fruit bowl out weighed 13 pounds less than people who didn't.

Another tactic: Keep your kitchen as squeaky clean as possible. In a separate study published in the journal *Environment & Behavior*,[3] women were placed in either an orderly kitchen or a messy one and asked to complete a writing task that had them describe a time they felt out of control, or that had them recount a time they felt in control, or that was neutral. The women were presented with snacks after each writing assignment. The participants in the chaotic kitchen ate almost three times as many calories from cookies when they were in the out-of-control mind-set than when they felt in control. The writing assignment did not affect what they ate in the clean kitchen, indicating that a disorganized environment

time you open the freezer. My trick is to buy junk foods that my family likes and I don't care that much about. They want Fudge Stripes and Ritz crackers? Great, I can avoid those things without too much trouble.

can contribute to overeating if you are feeling vulnerable.

Create a Pound-Shedding Pantry

Now that you've ditched the crap, you have plenty of room on your shelves for foods that can help you lose weight. But before you dash off to a big-box store to stock up on economy-size cases of healthy staples, remember that research[4] shows that when people stockpile food, they tend to eat more. Either keep those 3-gallon tubs of snacks out of sight and out of mind—or divide the munchies into smaller portions. Here's what you need in your pantry right now.

- Steel-cut oatmeal. Like regular rolled oats, steel-cut ones (which are more coarsely chopped) pack 6 grams of protein and 4 grams of fiber and contain 10 percent of your RDA of iron. But steel-cut oats are slightly lower in calories (140 versus 160 per $1/4$ dry cup) and take a little longer to digest, which keeps you feeling fuller.

- Natural nutrition bars with 5 grams (or less) of sugar. As someone who is short on time and long on sweet tooth, I could write a whole book about my love of nutrition bars. However, most "nutrition" bars are no better than a candy bar—loaded with calories, sugar, carbs, and sketchy chemicals. I have discovered two delicious all-natural, low-sugar bars that satisfy my sweet cravings. The Dark Chocolate, Nuts & Sea Salt KIND bar contains 6 grams of protein, 5 grams of sugar, and 7 grams of fiber for 200 calories. The NuGo Slim Raspberry Truffle has 17 grams of protein, 2 grams of sugar, and 7 grams of fiber for 180 calories. LÄRABAR bars work, too; they have more sugar than my two favorites, but the fat and fiber content can help keep you feeling satisfied.

- Fiber crackers. Fiber crackers tend to be lower in calories than other kinds of crackers; they're dense, so it takes longer to eat them; and the fiber fills you up fast (more on fiber in Chapter 4). My pick: GG Bran Crispbread, which contain only wheat bran, whole grain rye flour, and salt. Each giant cracker is only 25 calories and has 4 grams of fiber, and while they aren't as yummy as, say, Wheat Thins, they can satisfy a craving to crunch.

- Canned tuna (packed in water). Foodies may turn up their noses at canned tuna, but it's packed with heart-healthy omega-3 fatty acids, contains 16 grams of protein, is low in calories (there are just 70 in a 3-ounce can), and doesn't require any prep or cooking. Choose light tuna because it has about half as much mercury as albacore—and toss it on top of a salad or pile it on a slice of sprouted grain bread.

- Nuts. There's a reason nutritionists are nuts for nuts: They contain protein,

"I Did It!"

KATRINA'S STORY: When Katrina became a vegetarian in high school, she filled the void with carbs. "I ate a lot of white, starchy things," she says. Later, she got a job as an elementary school teacher and started eating out more, which led to more weight gain.

NAME: **Katrina McCloud**

AGE: **36**

HOMETOWN: **Waddell, Arizona**

BEFORE WEIGHT: **220**

AFTER WEIGHT: **145**

WAKE-UP CALL: Katrina, who is normally upbeat, had a meltdown in the dressing room of a plus-size clothing store. "I was spending a bunch of money on clothes I didn't even like. I hated looking at pictures of myself," she says. "My body didn't match who I was."

SUCCESS SECRETS: At her very next meal, Katrina started counting calories and monitoring portion sizes. Over time, she swapped processed white bread and pasta for whole grains and vegetables. After shedding 40 pounds, she added morning runs, cut dairy from her diet, and joined a gym. "I try to take as many classes at the gym as possible," she says. Now, Katrina's scale settles at 145 pounds. "I feel alive and confident, and like me again," she says.

unsaturated fat (which lowers "bad" cholesterol), omega-3s, fiber, and vitamin E (which prevents plaque buildup in your arteries).

- Canned beans. Beans are nutrient powerhouses. Take black beans, for example. Half a cup contains 8 grams of protein, 128 milligrams of folic acid, 2 grams of iron, 60 milligrams of magnesium, 306 milligrams of potassium, and 120 milligrams of phosphorus (which helps the body use carbs and fat and improves kidney function). Add them to soups and salads, or have them as a side with dinner.

- White wine vinegar. Scan the label of a bottle of salad dressing, and you'll be shocked at what you see: stuff like sugar, high-fructose corn syrup, and creepy-sounding artificial flavors. Douse your salad with white wine vinegar and olive oil instead; this type of vinegar has a milder flavor and less sugar and fewer calories than balsamic.

- Microwave popcorn. Yeah, microwave popcorn is old school—the smell brings me back to my college dorm room—but you can eat a ton of it (3½ cups!) for minimal calories (just 130). Plus, because you have to take the time to nuke it, it's not the kind of snack you're going to grab a handful of every time you pass by your pantry. Try Newman's Own Natural, which contains all healthy ingredients.

- Whole grains. People think you can't eat carbs when you're trying to lose weight, but you can—and you should! You just want to pick the right ones. Whole grains like brown rice, quinoa, and teff pack protein, fiber, and other important nutrients. (Teff, for example, is rich in calcium, vitamin C, and iron.)

- Protein powder. I'm not a smoothie person. These drinks can be loaded with calories (depending on what you chuck in there), and they're over too fast. In other words, I'd find it more satisfying to sit down and have a banana, a cup of berries, ¼ cup of yogurt, and a mound of steamed kale instead of blending it all together and sucking it down in 2 minutes. But many people love the taste and convenience of smoothies. To boost the nutrition profile, add a scoop of whey protein powder, which is milk based and higher in amino acids than other types of powder. If you have trouble digesting dairy, opt for pea protein powder instead, which contains about the same amount of protein.

STEP #2: HOLD YOURSELF ACCOUNTABLE

If someone asked you to recount everything you've eaten today, could you do it? And when I say everything, I mean every nibble of your kid's leftover mac and cheese, every lick of icing off a cupcake, and every taste of the chicken and rice dish you had while cooking it for dinner. Calories add up fast, and we have a way of conveniently forgetting all of the nibbling, tasting, and munching we do throughout the day, which means that we grossly underestimate how much we are really consuming.

TEST YOUR FOOD IQ

You may be surprised to find out that some meals, snacks, and drinks contain more (or in some cases, fewer) calories than you might think. Take a guess at how many calories are in each of the following items. (Find answers at the bottom.)

1 apple

1 slice thin-crust cheese pizza

1 frozen margarita

2 tablespoons peanut butter

1 slice whole wheat bread

1 California avocado

1 cup granola

1 ear corn

1 large baked potato

½ cup cookies & cream ice cream

Answers: Apple, 95; pizza, 123; margarita, at least 250; peanut butter, 190; bread, 70; avocado, 227; granola, 560 (varies by brand and type); corn, 88; potato, 278; ice cream, 160 (varies by brand)

Keep a food diary to record everything you are eating. (Research that appeared in the *American Journal of Preventive Medicine*[5] shows that keeping a daily diary can *double* a person's weight loss.) It doesn't have to be anything fancy. Simply note it on your phone or computer or jot it down in a notebook. (See the "Food Diary" sidebar on page 21 for more details.) DJ Gray, 37, of Lilly, Pennsylvania, wrote down everything she ate and tracked her calories with the SparkPeople app, which helped her lose 115 pounds. Popular calorie-tracking apps include MyFitnessPal, My Macros+, and FitDay. Going public can also help. Christina Donatella, 29, of Barrie, Ontario, set up a Facebook page to help hold herself accountable. It worked—she dropped 180 pounds. Christina now works as a personal trainer, motivating her clients through her Facebook page.

Weighing yourself is another way to stay honest. I know people who dread stepping on the scale more than root canals, colonoscopies, and bikini waxes put together. But it's essential for tracking your progress. Your friends and family may swear you don't look like you've gained a pound, but the scale doesn't lie. Most experts tout the benefits of weighing yourself once a week, but a new body of research reveals that daily weigh-ins are more effective. In a study from the *International Journal of Obesity*,[6] researchers found that people who weighed themselves at least 6 days a week for 12 months felt more

KILL A CRAVING

Experiencing a craving is sort of like being attacked by a shark—it comes out of nowhere, grabs onto you, and won't let go. When a craving strikes, there are two ways to beat it back. The first option: Distract yourself. Instead of reaching for the food you want, call a friend, answer an e-mail, take a shower, or go for a walk around the block.

The urge will likely pass by the time you're done. If it doesn't, ask yourself the following questions: "Am I really hungry?" "Will I really enjoy this?" "Is this something special that I don't get to have all the time?" "Have I been pretty good about eating a healthy diet and exercising regularly lately?" If you can answer, "yes" to all of those questions,

go ahead—eat it and enjoy every bite! The process of answering, "no" to some or all of the questions will reinforce the reasons why this craving isn't worth indulging, and chances are the craving will subside. Not always, but most of the time—and when it comes to slimming down and shaping up, most of the time is what matters.

confident about their ability to avoid overeating than those who stepped on the scale less frequently. Another study, published in the *Journal of Obesity*,[7] showed that participants who weighed themselves daily and tracked their weights on a Web site lost more weight in 1 year than those told to try to lose weight any way they wanted.

Initially, you may melt off a pound or more each week, and then the loss might slow down a bit. Also, the needle may stop moving as you gain muscle mass in place of fat (as you've already learned in this book, muscle weighs more than fat). Don't get discouraged! If you stick to the Take It All Off Plan, I promise you will bust through plateaus and keep losing.

How to Keep a Food Diary

Here are the rules: Write down everything you eat or drink from the moment you wake up until you hit the sack at night (that

includes bites of cookies, sticks of gum, every french fry snuck off your husband's plate). Be as specific as you can about the portion size and ingredients in each meal, snack, or stolen bite; jot down where you ate it, why you ate it, and how you felt after you chowed it down. Aim to do this for at least 3 days to help identify any potential diet-derailing patterns. See the sample 1-day diary (opposite).

STEP #3: TEAM UP

We naturally mirror the behaviors of those around us. If you're out to dinner with a crowd of junk-food eaters, you'll tend to order (and polish off) a large unhealthy meal because it will feel socially acceptable to do so; conversely, if you're dining with another dieter, you'll feel too guilty to order fried calamari as your appetizer and get the side salad instead. Studies bear this out: When

Food Diary DATE: AUGUST 2, 2016

TIME OF DAY	FOOD EATEN & AMOUNT/ MEASURE	PREPARATION METHOD/ DESCRIPTION	LOCATION	WHY YOU ATE IT	HOW YOU FELT AFTER EATING IT
7:00 a.m.	2 scrambled eggs 1 slice whole wheat toast 1 cup of coffee	Eggs were cooked in a pan with olive oil cooking spray; toast was dry/no butter; dash of skim milk and 1 packet of Splenda in coffee	At home	Breakfast	Satisfied
9:30 a.m.	1 KIND bar 16-oz bottle of water		At work	Was getting a little hungry	Not hungry anymore
11:30 a.m.	Handful of almonds 16-oz bottle of water	Raw	At work	There was a bag of them sitting on my desk, and I felt like eating them	Not hungry
1:30 p.m.	Cobb salad with chicken, tomato, avocado, bacon, hard-cooked eggs, and house dressing Seltzer with lemon	Chicken was grilled; regular full-fat dressing	At restaurant with coworkers	Lunch	Satisfied
3:30 p.m.	16-oz iced coffee	Mixed with skim milk (not sure how much was put in)	At a coffee shop, during a break from work	Bored	Neutral (not particularly hungry or not hungry)
5:00 p.m.	Handful of M&M's 1 diet soda		At work	Was craving something sweet and a little bloated	Still craving sweets!
7:30 p.m.	6-oz piece of salmon with ½ cup brown rice and ¾ cup cooked spinach 1 very full glass of sauvignon blanc	Salmon was grilled with ½ tablespoon olive oil and salt and pepper; spinach was steamed	At home	Dinner	Full
9:00 p.m.	1 scoop low-fat vanilla ice cream		At home	Dessert	Happy!

researchers at the Cornell University Food and Brand Lab[8] had study subjects eat a meal with an actress wearing a "fat suit," they ate about 32 percent more pasta and roughly 43 percent less salad than participants who ate with the actress when she wasn't wearing the extra padding. So when you're trying to lose weight, it's best to hang (or at least dine) with like-minded people who support and share your goals.

The same holds true for exercise. To increase motivation and accountability and boost the fun factor, many of the women you'll be meeting in this book started working out with a friend, spouse, or family member. You'll be more likely to go on a morning jog if you know there's someone waiting at the park to meet you.

"You can't make excuses when people are counting on you to exercise with them," says Ontario native Andrea Tynkaluk. This tactic helped her sweat off 43 pounds. Other options include joining a training group, which offers the same kind of pack mentality (plus, training groups tend to have set workout schedules that can help you stay on track), or booking sessions with a trainer.

To boost your results, choose a workout partner who brings out your competitive side. In a study from *Annals of Behavioral Medicine,*[9] researchers asked female college students to exercise on a stationary bike for as long as they could. The participants, on average, peddled for 10 minutes. In the next phase

NAME: **Andrea Tynkaluk**
AGE: **35**
HOMETOWN: **Ontario**
BEFORE WEIGHT: **190**
AFTER WEIGHT: **147**

of the study, the researchers told the subjects they were working out with a partner in another lab who had previously ridden the bike for 40 percent longer than they had. Guess what happened? The participants

"I Did It!"

BRITTANY'S STORY: When Brittany met her boyfriend, Gabe, in high school, they were both overweight—and they packed on more pounds together. "We'd make frozen foods like egg rolls and pizza rolls," says Brittany. After quitting sports because she felt self-conscious about her weight at practice, her only exercise consisted of "walking to the car to go get fast food." As a senior in college, she wore size 20 jeans.

NAME: **Brittany Blankenship**
AGE: **26**
HOMETOWN: **Lafayette, Indiana**
BEFORE WEIGHT: **248**
AFTER WEIGHT: **155**

WAKE-UP CALL: In September 2011, Brittany was a bridesmaid in a friend's wedding. When she saw the photos, she was horrified. She weighed herself for the first time in almost 2 years, and the number—248—shocked her. "There is no way I am going to hit 250," she promised herself.

SUCCESS SECRETS: That October, she and Gabe started taking walks and doing daily workouts they found on Pinterest. In July 2012, they started doing a different yoga video every day. At the same time, the pair swore off fast food and switched their drinks from soda and juices to water and unsweetened tea. In 9 months, Brittany dropped 30 pounds. "My new snacks are apples, carrots, and celery," says Brittany. Now, she and Gabe jog 3 or more miles 3 days a week, do yoga videos 3 other days, and "walk the mall" on Saturdays. She is down to 155 and has launched a career as a chef, specializing in good-for-you gourmet. "I love finding healthy ways to make old favorites," she says.

upped their ride times by 9 minutes. In the last phase, the researchers told the subjects that they were now working together with a partner to get a team score. The subjects rose to the occasion and peddled for 2 minutes longer than they had when they weren't working out in a team scenario. The moral of this story: Working out with someone fitter than you boosts motivation.

STEP #4: STRESS LESS AND SLEEP MORE

When you eat the right things and exercise like famous trainer Jillian Michaels yet still can't shake extra pounds, your hormones may be to blame, specifically cortisol. Cortisol, referred to as the stress hormone, is primarily triggered by anxiety and sleep deprivation, and numerous studies have shown that it contributes to abdominal fat storage. When you're under stress (sleep deprivation counts as stress because it strains your system), your body starts cranking out cortisol, which releases fat from fat stores and dumps it into the bloodstream to provide your organs with energy to fight off the perceived threat. Whatever fat isn't used gets re-stored in abdominal fat tissue, which contains four times more cortisol receptors than fat storage units in other areas of the body. When you're under chronic stress, your body gets paranoid that you're going to run out of fuel, so it keeps cortisol levels elevated. And here's the worst part: The more belly fat you have, the more cortisol you produce. When stress simmers down, lingering cortisol becomes inactive and flushed out of the body. But fat tissue can literally switch it back on before your body has the chance to get rid of it.

It's vital to get this hormone under control so it doesn't undermine the results you'll achieve on this program. Blow off steam by practicing yoga, meditating, exercising (working out improves cortisol sensitivity, meaning you pump out less of the hormone when stressed and levels drop back down to normal faster after the stressful situation has been resolved)—or simply doing anything you personally find relaxing (reading a book, watching Bravo, shopping online—you get the picture). And get plenty of shut-eye! If you can't squeeze in the recommended 8 hours a night, try taking an afternoon snooze. Research from Pennsylvania State University[10] shows that a 2-hour midafternoon nap can reverse the cortisol effects of a poor night's sleep. I know what you're thinking: Who the hell has time for a *2-hour nap*?! Fortunately, shorter siestas can help, too—every little bit counts!

TIPS TO GO

Whew! That was a lot of info, right? While it may seem like much goes into Taking It All Off, it really boils down to these five simple, failproof strategies. Refer to them whenever you are struck with self-doubt or temptation.

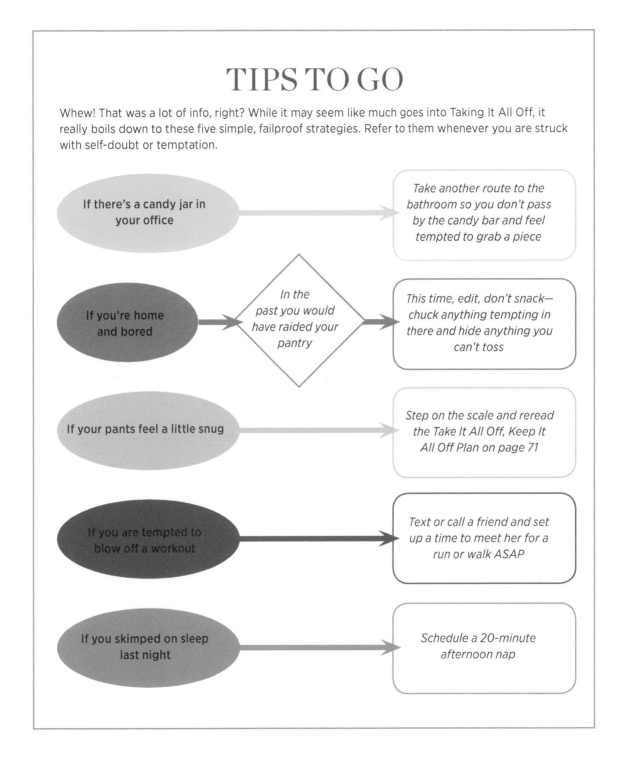

If there's a candy jar in your office → *Take another route to the bathroom so you don't pass by the candy bar and feel tempted to grab a piece*

If you're home and bored → *In the past you would have raided your pantry* → *This time, edit, don't snack—chuck anything tempting in there and hide anything you can't toss*

If your pants feel a little snug → *Step on the scale and reread the Take It All Off, Keep It All Off Plan on page 71*

If you are tempted to blow off a workout → *Text or call a friend and set up a time to meet her for a run or walk ASAP*

If you skimped on sleep last night → *Schedule a 20-minute afternoon nap*

Easy Ways to
Eat Less

There are all kinds of diets out there—and while each one is based on a specific weight loss philosophy, they are all essentially trying to get you to do the same thing: eat less. (Even those low-carb diets that encourage you to chow on endless amounts of red meat are betting that you aren't going to take down three porterhouse steaks like you would three pieces of cake.) The Take It All Off Plan isn't based on a popular trend. As the women who made this book possible can attest, if you follow the plan and eat healthier, eat a little less, and pay attention to how many calories you're taking in, you *will* lose weight.

Calorie counting isn't trendy, but it works. Do you have any idea how many calories you've consumed so far today? If you're like most people, you haven't a clue. Keeping track of the caloric value of what you put in your mouth and doing some mental tallying throughout the day will help you make smarter food decisions. For example, if you've eaten a lot of calories by midafternoon, you'll know to have a smaller dinner. If you don't go crazy at dinner, you might be able to afford a small dessert. Keeping tabs on calories (and making adjustments to compensate for splurges) is the secret to losing weight—and preventing it from creeping back on. The women here came up with some simple and super helpful calorie-cutting strategies. I'll be revealing their tricks, plus giving you portion-control pointers, self-control strategies—and more!

POLICE YOUR PORTIONS

The first step to shedding pounds is to practice portion control. The key word here is *control*. The obvious way to do this is to simply eat half of what is on your plate or serve yourself half as much as you typically would take. Unfortunately, most of us have trouble doing this (um, guilty!), so you need to get creative. One way is to use smaller bowls, smaller spoons, and dessert plates in place of dinner plates—all of which trick you into thinking you are eating more than you really are. A clever study in the *American Journal of Preventive Medicine*[1] looked at how much ice cream a group of nutritionists served themselves at an ice cream social. Some of the nutrition experts were given a 17-ounce bowl, while others were handed a 34-ounce bowl. The big bowl group served themselves 31 percent more ice cream than the nutritionists given smaller bowls— and their servings increased by 14.5 percent

NAME: **Jen Punda**

AGE: **33**

HOMETOWN: **Bolingbrook, Illinois**

BEFORE WEIGHT: **230**

AFTER WEIGHT: **139**

when they were offered larger ice cream scoopers. If nutritionists are duped by big bowls and utensils, how can there be any hope for the rest of us? But of course there is, as our Take It All Off heroes have proven.

SIZE MATTERS

HERE'S WHAT PROPER PORTIONS OF COMMON FOODS SHOULD LOOK LIKE.

AVOCADO: Pack of Trident gum

BUTTER: Bottle cap

CHEESE: Four stacked dice

DICED WATERMELON: Soup can

GRAINS LIKE QUINOA OR BROWN RICE:
Tennis ball

GRANOLA: Plastic Easter egg

HUMMUS: Hockey puck

MEAT, POULTRY, ANY FISH BUT SALMON:
Your (whole) hand

OLIVE OIL: Poker chip

PEANUT BUTTER: Ping-Pong ball

RAISINS: Golf ball

SALMON: A checkbook

TOFU: Bar of soap

Another important element of the Take It All Off Plan is learning to identify healthy portion sizes. Jen Punda, 33, of Bolingbrook, Illinois, downloaded the MyFitnessPal app to help gauge her portions, and she dropped 91 pounds; Krystal Sanders invested in a portion-control plate; and DJ Gray bought a food scale. As the size of their meals shrank, so did the size of their bodies. An easy method for judging portions is to compare food servings to common household items. See the "Size Matters" sidebar for visual comparisons.

BREAK OUT YOUR APRON

In addition to watching your portions, you need to keep a keen eye on your calories. The best way to do this is to cook at home instead of eating out.

Eating at home helps you save calories, eat more healthily, and lose weight. Research from the journal *Public Health Nutrition*[2] showed that people who cooked most of their meals consumed less calories, carbs, sugar, and fat than those who cooked infrequently or not at all. What's more, those who cooked dinner at home most nights each week consumed fewer calories even on the rare occasions when they ate dinner out than noncooks did. Cooking puts you in control of the ingredients—and makes you more aware of what's in restaurant dishes (lots and lots of oil and butter!), so you know what to avoid.

You can easily recreate restaurant faves at home, using healthier ingredients. For example, Katie Russell, who lost 93 pounds, put the kibosh on Chinese takeout and started making her own healthy stir-fries with kale, quinoa, and tofu.

SNEAKY SWAPS

Dropping pounds doesn't mean you can *never* eat out. What would be the fun in that? Here are tasty stand-ins for beloved restaurant meals as well as your go-to recipes.

At a Restaurant

Instead of chicken parm, order chicken paillard—Ditching the breading, cheese, and most of the oil can save you over 700 calories and 35 grams of fat.

Instead of a beef burrito, order beef tacos—Rice, steak, cheese, and sour cream can put your burrito into the 500-calorie range. Tacos (beef, lettuce, tomato, cheese, and salsa stuffed into a flour taco shell) ring in at around 260 calories.

Instead of a Cobb salad, order a grilled chicken salad—Loaded with chicken, cheese, avocado, bacon, eggs, and creamy dressing, a Cobb salad can cost you calories. Even when sprinkled with a little cheese and doused with honey-lime vinaigrette, a grilled chicken salad is a respectable (and nondiet-derailing) 260 calories.

Instead of kung pao shrimp, order steamed shrimp with veggies—Thanks to the sweet-sour-spicy sauce, kung pao rings in at 840 calories and 52 grams of fat. To kick up the flavor profile of the steamed version, add a little soy sauce and a dash of hot mustard.

Instead of a rib eye steak, order filet mignon—This lean, delicate cut has only 218 calories and 9 grams of fat per typical 6-ounce portion, compared to the 544 calories and 35 grams of fat you'll find in a 10-ounce rib eye.

In the Kitchen

Here are some simple ways to skinny up home-cooked comfort foods.

Instead of pasta, try spaghetti squash—A cup of cooked spaghetti has 220 calories and 43 grams of carbs. One cup of spaghetti squash (which is similar in taste and appearance to actual spaghetti) has only 42 calories and 10 grams of carbs. Nuke or bake the squash until you can scrape "noodles" out with a fork, and top with marinara sauce.

Instead of mashed potatoes, try mashed cauliflower—This delicious spin on mashed spuds contains only 80 calories, 1 gram of fat, and 12 grams of carbs per half cup.

Instead of bread, try lettuce leaves—Save yourself dozens of calories by placing sandwich fixings in a big piece of lettuce, instead of between two slices of bread.

Instead of oil, try unsweetened applesauce—In most baked goods recipes, you can use applesauce in place of oil without anyone noticing the difference. (If you're a risk-taker, you can also try subbing tofu, black beans, or avocado for oil.) Mixing in applesauce instead of oil can save you nearly 1,000 calories per batch of brownies.

Instead of white flour, try almond flour—"Bread" chicken cutlets and fish fillets with this gluten-free flour sub that contains protein, healthy fats, and 10 percent of the RDA for vitamin E. It contains 160 calories, 6 grams of carbs, and 14 grams of fat per ¼ cup.

NAME: **Katie Russell**

AGE: **34**

HOMETOWN: **Edmond, Oklahoma**

BEFORE WEIGHT: **230**

AFTER WEIGHT: **137**

I know what you're thinking: *But I don't have time to cook!* If you're super busy, steal this trick from Jessie Foss of Garland, Texas, who shed 100 pounds: Whip up a big batch of something healthy, like soup in a slow cooker, on a Sunday, when you have extra time, and eat it throughout the week. Annie Allen cooks healthy meals like baked fish on her days off so she can bring leftovers to work for lunch.

When you eat out, be careful. Dining at fast-food restaurants is a fast way to gain weight. Just ask Zakiee Labib, 35, from Westlake, Ohio, who was hitting the drive-thru at least 4 nights a week, driving her weight up to 200 pounds, and Christina Donatella, whose frequent fast-food meals landed her at 380 pounds. Sit-down restaurants typically offer more variety and healthier ingredients, but portions tend to be gigantic, and, of course, if you're paying for something, you feel like you should eat it, right? Researchers at Tufts University[3] discovered that in 123 restaurants in three cities one meal (without drinks, apps, or dessert) sometimes exceeded one's recommended caloric intake for an entire day. (In case you're interested, American, Chinese, and Italian eateries had the highest calorie counts per meal—around 1,495). So save yourself cash and calories and eat at home.

COOK ONCE, EAT FOR A WEEK

Roast a chicken on Sunday, and then toss the cooked poultry and veggies into your meals until Friday.

Sunday: Roast a chicken with carrots, onions, and sweet potatoes (brush the bird with 1 tablespoon olive oil and sprinkle with salt and pepper; set the chicken in a roasting pan, surround with veggies chopped into large pieces, and cook at 425°F for about 1½ hours)

Monday: Sliced chicken sandwich with lettuce and tomato on sprouted grain bread

Tuesday: Mixed Greens Salad (page 92) with chicken breast

Wednesday: Mock Chicken Fried Rice (see page 121, but add the cooked chicken in at the end with the eggs, rice, and peas, as opposed to cooking the chicken in an earlier step)

Thursday: Scrambled eggs with sweet potato "hash" (chop the cooked sweet potatoes into 1-inch pieces, and then warm them in a cast-iron skillet; sprinkle with red-pepper flakes to taste, and garnish with chopped scallions; serve with scrambled eggs)

Friday: Chicken noodle soup (pour five 14.5-ounce cans of chicken broth into a large pot and add the chicken, chopped veggies, 1 package tofu shirataki noodles prepared according to package instructions, ½ teaspoon basil, ½ teaspoon oregano, and salt and pepper to taste; bring to a boil and then simmer for about 20 minutes)

SNACK SMARTER

Constant snacking is a bad habit; strategic snacking can be a good one. In the Take It All Off Plan, you will be eating a protein-rich snack in the morning and one in the afternoon to help keep your blood sugar stable, which will prevent you from overeating during meals. When it comes to snacking, it's important to plan ahead. You get in trouble when hunger strikes at 3:00 p.m., and the only option is the office vending machine. Or you're on the road and there's nothing for miles but fast-food restaurants. Stash portion-controlled packages of healthy snacks in your desk, car, or purse so you have something nutritious on hand when you feel the urge to eat. Donesha Bolden of Atlanta, Georgia, who lost 100 pounds, says, "I keep zip-top bags handy for snacks like grapes, celery, and cucumbers." Zakiee Labib always has a healthy snack, like an apple, in the car. Bridget Rauschenberg carries around veggies, trail mix, and string cheese. As long as you're armed with good-for-you munchies (like fruit, veggies, Greek yogurt, nuts, hard-cooked eggs, and healthy nutrition bars), you won't blow your diet.

"I Did It!"

BRITTANY'S STORY: As a teenager, Brittany loved going out with friends for pizza, tacos, or chicken and French fries. "I would get every dipping sauce—the barbecue, the ranch, you name it," says Brittany. She played sports, but it wasn't enough to offset her junk-food-heavy diet. By high school graduation, Brittany, who is 5 feet 4 inches, weighed nearly 250 pounds.

NAME: **Brittany Hicks**

AGE: **25**

HOMETOWN: **Carson, California**

BEFORE WEIGHT: **247**

AFTER WEIGHT: **137**

WAKE-UP CALL: As a second-semester college freshman, Brittany ventured to the gym for the first time since high school—and crossed paths with a personal trainer. "She gave me her card and told me to call her when I was ready for a change," says Brittany. "I was curious. Could I really lose weight?" Months later, a few days after her 20th birthday, she decided it was time to find out, and she made the call.

SUCCESS SECRETS: Twice a week for an hour, Brittany lunged, ran stairs, and lifted dumbbells with her trainer. She started a food journal, paying attention to what she ate—and why. After a few weeks, she was down 10 pounds. She cleaned up her diet (Greek yogurt and granola for breakfast; protein and veggies for lunch and dinner) and shed another 35 pounds in 4 months. As she approached the 100-pound mark, she wrote her goal weight, 147, on her wrist for inspiration—and she reached it right before her 21st birthday. Since then, she's dropped 10 more pounds! Now, the 25-year-old social worker stays in shape by trying different fitness classes or running a 5-K every week with her coworkers. "We always find a fun adventure to go on!" she says.

BEWARE HEALTH FOODS!

A New York City nutritionist once told me that many of his fancy clients were getting fat from shopping at a certain health food store. I was shocked. *How could health food stores be making people gain weight?* Well, it turns out that many foods with health halos are actually packed with calories, sugar, and other fattening stuff—and because we consider them virtuous, we tend to eat them with abandon. Take nuts, for example. An ounce of almonds (about 23 nuts) has 14 grams of fat and more than 160 calories. Good luck sticking to just 1 ounce when you're eating them out of a 1-pound pouch from Trader Joe's. Hummus has 80 calories per 2-tablespoon serving, and I have been known to polish off an entire tub with the help of some baby carrot dippers. Whole grains like quinoa and farro are nutritious, but we tend to eat mountains of them, and the calories add up fast. (A cup can have up to 220 calories.)

Even fruit can be fattening. A cup of grapes has 23 grams of sugar, which is 13 more grams than three Chips Ahoy! cookies. Tropical fruits like pineapple, mango, and bananas are high in sugar, too.

Be especially careful with gluten-free packaged foods, which can also be high in the sweet stuff. Hannah Casey, 34, of Charleston, South Carolina, suffers from celiac disease, but she doesn't use it as an excuse to eat end-

NAME: **Hannah Casey**

AGE: **34**

HOMETOWN: **Charleston, South Carolina**

BEFORE WEIGHT: **248**

AFTER WEIGHT: **137**

less amounts of gluten-free goodies. "I lost weight because I stopped eating cookies all the time," Hannah says. "Not because I just started eating gluten-free cookies."

The lesson here? Even with healthy, whole foods, practice portion control! Buy 100-calorie packs of almonds, and when you eat hummus, scoop out a serving and put the rest of the tub away in the fridge. And when you are counting every last calorie, let your bowl of grapes live in the back of the refrigerator—out of sight, out of mind, out of mouth.

BOOST YOUR WILLPOWER

In a famous 1960s study, a team of researchers at Stanford University asked preschoolers if they would rather have one marshmallow now or wait a few minutes while the researcher left the room and have two marshmallows when the researcher returned. Researchers followed up with the participants 40 years later and found that the children who were able to delay gratification in the study fared better in life—and, by the way, also had lower BMIs.[4]

Some people naturally have more willpower than others, but you can grow your self-control by developing good habits. Here are three key ways.

Think ahead. People who struggle with self-control tend to live in the moment. Research[5] has shown that imagining positive future events (an upcoming vacation or family reunion, for example) can dilute the impulse to polish off a plate of cookies in front of you. Makes sense to me. First, it serves as a distraction—if you can get your mind off the cookies for a few minutes, the urge to eat them will likely pass. Second, it gets you thinking about the consequences of eating those cookies. In other words, how you'll look and feel at that special event if you keep eating junk food.

A study that appeared in the journal *Appetite*[6] found that this mental trick was especially effective when study participants were told to focus on a food-related scenario. The subjects who were prompted to think about what they had for lunch or what they planned to have for dinner before having a snack consumed less than those told to imagine non-eating experiences. I do this all the time. When I crave cheese at 4:00 p.m., as I often do, I think about what I have already eaten that day and what I am planning to eat for dinner—and this makes me take the time to consider if I can spare the calories on this snack. Sometimes I can. If I had a big lunch or plan to go out for dinner, I can't. And I (usually!) don't. Hey, no one's perfect.

Avoid stressful situations. You only have so much self-control, research shows, so you want to save it for when you really need it. A study published in the journal *Psychological Science*[7] found that dieters have more luck saying no to unhealthy foods if they avoid situations that test their

"I Did It!"

ALEXANDRA'S STORY: A lifelong athlete, Alexandra always worked out three times a week—but it wasn't enough to make up for her oversize eating habits. "I usually ate pretty healthy, but I also ate a lot," says the fashion designer.

WAKE-UP CALL: "I saw bridesmaid pics from my best friend's wedding," says Alexandra. "I couldn't believe I had gotten to that point."

NAME: **Alexandra Shipper**
AGE: **28**
HOMETOWN: **New York, New York**
BEFORE WEIGHT: **200**
AFTER WEIGHT: **145**

SUCCESS SECRETS: Alexandra usually shied away from group fitness classes, but she finally got up the guts in 2012 to sign up for a kettlebell class—and was immediately hooked. She started using a calorie-counting guide to shrink her portions and nixed packaged foods, dropping 30 pounds in 6 months. Her diet soon included staples like egg whites, fish, homemade green juices, and healthy fats like avocado. Later in 2012, Alexandra started taking classes at her local SoulCycle studio and soon added SLT (Strengthen-Lengthen-Tone) and boot camp classes to her schedule. By April 2013, she had run her first half-marathon, and in 2016, she completed a half Ironman. "The way I feel without processed foods is extraordinary," says Alexandra, citing clearer skin and fewer headaches. And with a newfound sense of confidence to match the clothes she designs. "Life is just better," she says. "I don't have to settle for just any outfit that fits on my body."

self-control. (For example, now is not the time to swear off social media or resist browsing in stores you know you can't afford.) If you are constantly calling upon self-control to manage stress, and deal with temptation and other challenges, you won't have any left when you sit down to dinner, making you more apt to ravage the breadbasket.

In this study, chronic dieters were asked to complete a task—some of the tasks involved calling upon self-control and others didn't. Then the researchers scanned the dieters' brains while they looked at images of tantalizing high-calorie foods. The result: The dieters who had to call upon self-control during the task had more going on in the orbitofrontal cortex, the part of the brain associated with food rewards, and less connectivity between that area of the brain and the inferior frontal gyrus, which is responsible for self-control. Of course, it's impossible to completely dodge challenging situations, but the more you can reduce stress, the easier it will be to say no when you really need to.

Pay attention. People with willpower feel satiated faster than those with low self-control. And it's not always because they are hardwired to stop after a few crackers—they simply may pay more attention to how many crackers they are eating. (A University of Minnesota study[8] found that when subjects who struggled with self-control started counting their snacks, they became satiated faster, too.) To help keep tabs on your food intake, avoid eating while watching TV, checking your Twitter feed, or reading a magazine—distractions can make you forget how many crackers you're consuming until your fingers are scraping the bottom of the box. Also, flip the box over to see how many crackers constitute a serving, count that many out, and put the box away. If you like the freedom of eating out of a box (risky but satisfying for some people), count how many you pop in your mouth. Hearing yourself say a high number, like 20, will signal to your brain that it's time to start feeling full.

How to Stay Satiated

Hunger is our built-in gas gauge that alerts us when it's time to refuel. If we pay attention to it, our bodies get what they need and keep cruising along. If we drive around on empty, we break down—and plow through a sleeve of Oreos. On a well-balanced diet that's rich in filling protein and fiber—like the Take It All Off Plan in this book—you'll only feel hungry every 4 hours, when the nutrients that you consumed in your previous meal have been depleted and it's time to fill up your tank again. What you'll never feel is starving. That only happens when you aren't eating the right foods. More on that later.

The trouble is that most of us don't eat when we're hungry. Let me clarify: We *think* we're hungry, but what we are really feeling is tired, sad, happy, bored, or anxious. "I realized [by keeping a food journal] that I'd been using food to cope with stress," says Carson, California, native Brittany Hicks, who went on to drop

100 pounds. DJ Gray would soothe herself with comfort foods like meat loaf and mashed potatoes after pressure-filled days running a daycare business and mothering her own four kids.

So how do you know if you're truly hungry? There are a few telltale signs that come with authentic hunger.

- You have trouble concentrating.
- You're cranky.
- Your stomach literally feels empty.
- You crave food in general—not something specific like pizza or chocolate.

The goal is to eat until you feel *satiated*, which means you've removed the feeling of hunger while stopping long before you feel stuffed. Here's how to do that.

1. Midway through your meal, pause for a moment and ask yourself how full you are feeling on a scale of 1 to 10. When you hit around a 6 or 7, it's time to stop eating.

2. Take the opportunity to check in with your taste buds. Is the flavor of your food still irresistibly appetizing? If not, then you've had enough.

It may take a few meals for you to recognize when you are sated. But eventually you will automatically identify the feeling and stop eating at the right time.

Some strategies to increase satiety are:

1. Choose filling, low-calorie foods.
2. Kick off the day with a healthy breakfast.
3. Take pleasure in the taste of your food.

THE PROTEIN SWEET SPOT

Nutritionists, trainers . . . even your mother is probably telling you to eat more protein. And with good reason: Protein contains amino acids that aid in muscle production and repair, and it also helps keep bones strong and healthy. It's kind of a pain in the butt to digest, which means your body actually has to burn calories to move it through your system. And because this is a pretty slow process, you stay full for hours. So it's not surprising that research published in the *International Journal of Obesity*[1] showed that people on a high-protein diet (with 25 percent of their calories coming from protein) lost nearly double the amount of weight in 6 months than those on a higher-carb, lower-protein diet (with only 12 percent of daily calories coming from protein).[2]

But eating too much of the wrong kind of protein may hurt your health. A 2012 study in the *Archives of Internal Medicine*[3] found that consuming higher amounts of red meat (particularly processed red meat, like hot dogs and bacon) was linked to cancer and cardiovascular death, while replacing one serving of red meat with fish, poultry, nuts, legumes, or low-fat dairy lowered risk of death. Animal

PROTEIN CALCULATOR

IF YOU WEIGH . . .

130 pounds—you need at least 65 grams of protein per day

150 pounds—you need at least 75 grams of protein per day

175 pounds—you need at least 88 grams of protein per day

200 pounds—you need at least 100 grams of protein per day

225 pounds—you need at least 113 grams of protein per day

250 pounds—you need at least 125 grams of protein per day

proteins contain all nine essential amino acids in the proportions that your body needs, so opting for lean (nonprocessed) meat, poultry, fish, eggs, and dairy will protect your health *and* help you lose weight. Vegetarians and vegans can still reap the benefits by eating plant-based sources of protein, like beans, nuts, and grains. The trick is to combine two or more of them at every meal (like oatmeal topped with almonds, for example) to ensure you're getting in all of your aminos. Just keep in mind that plant-based sources aren't as protein dense as animal sources, so you need to eat more of them to get enough of the nutrient—and as we know from the previous chapter, calories in healthy foods can add up fast. Be careful!

So how much protein should you eat per day? If you're regularly working up a sweat, as you will be on the Take It All Off Plan, you'll need around 0.5 to 0.7 gram of protein per pound of body weight to help maintain and repair all that sexy new muscle. So a 150-pound woman needs at least 75 grams a day, ideally spread out over three large meals, or three smaller meals and two snacks. Muscle breakdown occurs throughout the day, so you need a steady stream of the nutrient to deal with the constant damage.

MORE FIBER, PLEASE

Fiber is the Khloé Kardashian of nutrients— once overlooked and overshadowed, it's now the hottest thing since sliced (sprouted grain) bread. Researchers at the University of Massachusetts Medical School[4] asked one group of volunteers to follow the American Heart Association's (AHA) diet for preventing heart disease, which advises eating fruit, veggies, high-fiber foods, and lean protein—and going easy on salt, sugar, fat, and booze. Another group of participants were just asked to eat 30 grams of fiber per day. Both groups shed pounds and lowered blood pressure. The AHA group lost a little more weight (5.9 pounds versus 4.6 pounds) than the fiber-only dieters, but both successfully kept it off for a year. The cool thing here is that doing nothing other than eating more fiber resulted in nearly as much weight loss as an entire diet overhaul. Let's ponder that for a moment.

Fiber is the part of the plant that your body can't digest, so you don't absorb any calories from it. There are two types: Insoluble fiber helps shuttle food through your digestive system, and soluble fiber's job description includes slowing the digestion of sugar and fat, which keeps energy levels high and blood sugar levels stable. What's more, fiber expands in your stomach, making you feel fuller, and fiber-filled foods are denser, tricking you into thinking you're eating more calories than you are.

Good sources of fiber include oatmeal and cereals like Fiber One or All-Bran; whole grains like brown rice, barley, and quinoa; veggies like broccoli and artichokes; fruits like pears, apples, and raspberries; beans; and nuts. The daily recommendation for fiber for women is 25 grams, and nailing that number is as easy as having a bowl of oatmeal with a half a cup of raspberries (8 grams) for breakfast and a cup of brown rice tossed with a cup of lentils (19 grams) for lunch.

Beware of juicing—most of a fruit's fiber lives in the pulp and the skin, so chucking those parts of the produce robs you of fiber.

GOOD FATS VERSUS BAD FATS

First fat was bad, and then it was good. Now fat is both bad and good. Confused yet? The "good" kinds can help lower LDL cholesterol levels. They include polyunsaturated fats, which are found in nuts, seeds, fatty fish, and vegetable oil, and monounsaturated fats, which reside in olive oil, nuts, seeds, and avocados. The "bad" kinds are saturated (found in foods like meat, cheese, and butter) and trans fats, which usually go by the name "partially hydrogenated oils" and pop up in fried foods and packaged baked goods. Both of these "bad" fats raise LDL levels, putting you at risk for heart disease and stroke.

Spiking your diet with good fats can help you lose weight, if they are eaten in moderation. (They have more calories per gram than protein or carbs, so you have to be extra careful about portion control.) Fat is dense and improves flavor, so eating food that contains fat is satisfying. It also gives you energy, aids in cell growth, protects your organs, and helps your body use certain nutrients.

DON'T FORGET TO EAT BREAKFAST

Breakfast is a bit of a hot-button issue. Some studies show it contributes to weight loss, while others do not. A review of research, published in *Obesity Reviews*,[5] showed a small

"I Did It!"

DONESHA'S STORY: As a kid, Donesha existed on chips, sugary drinks, burgers, and mayonnaise-y foods like potato salad. Her idea of dieting was to try not to eat all day—but she'd inevitably gorge when she got home. When Donesha moved from North Carolina to Atlanta for a teaching job, she weighed over 200 pounds and wore a size 24.

NAME: **Donesha Bolden**

AGE: **37**

HOMETOWN: **Atlanta, Georgia**

BEFORE WEIGHT: **220**

AFTER WEIGHT: **120**

WAKE-UP CALL: It was literally a call—alerting her that her 35-year-old cousin had passed away, and the cause of his death was high blood pressure due to obesity. Donesha realized these health risks ran in her family, and she became determined not to suffer the same fate.

SUCCESS SECRETS: Donesha started waking up early to run 3 miles before work. Then she'd hit the gym or the track in the evening. She learned to cook, whipping up tilapia and steamed broccoli and opting for baked sweet potatoes instead of salty bagged snacks. In 2 months, she lost 30 pounds. Donesha quit skipping breakfast and started each day with oatmeal and fruit, and she was down to 160 pounds by November 2012. She then bought a portion-control plate to keep tabs on how much she was eating and started lifting heavier weights during workouts. She now weighs in at a slender 120 pounds and uses her Instagram account to inspire others to get fit. "When a person tells me they want to look out for their health because they saw me do it, that's reward enough," she says.

amount of evidence linking skipping breakfast and obesity. In another study of obese women that appeared in the *American Journal of Clinical Nutrition*,[6] researchers put women on a weight loss plan. One group ate breakfast and the other didn't (daily calories for both groups remained the same). After 12 weeks, the breakfast group lost 20 pounds, while the skippers lost 14 pounds. The researchers speculate that eating breakfast slashes impulsive snacking, which—are you listening?—is essential for losing weight.

However, a study from Columbia University[7] questions the "breakfast is the most important meal of the day" theory. The researchers had one group of overweight people eat oatmeal for breakfast, had another eat frosted cornflakes, and had the last group skip breakfast. The breakfast skippers lost more weight after 4 weeks than either of the breakfast groups, because even if they did overdo it at lunch, they did not eat as many additional calories as if they'd had breakfast. They were still in calorie deficit.

So while the jury is still out in the research world, our own panel of successful weight loss candidates ate breakfast. So **eat breakfast, please.** (Brittany Hicks ate Greek yogurt and granola for breakfast; Donesha Bolden started kicking off her day with oatmeal and fruit; and Anu Sharma's a.m. meal was cottage cheese and berries.) In my opinion, one of the most important reasons to eat breakfast is that blowing off breakfast can have a danger-

ous domino effect. When the hunger kicks in around 11, you grab a muffin, which will make your blood sugar spike then crash, resulting in more hunger. So then you overeat at lunch. At that point it becomes, *Hell, I've already blown my diet today, so I might as well have a cupcake at the office party and a heaping bowl of pasta washed down with two glasses of Cabernet for dinner and start over again tomorrow!* Only for the exact same scenario to repeat itself the next day. Sound familiar? Another reason to eat in the a.m. is that we're not as likely to overeat at breakfast as we are at other meals (boozy weekend brunches being the exception). Plus, breakfast sets the tone for the rest of the day. Choosing something healthy like yogurt, eggs, or oatmeal gives you an incentive to keep up the good work.

WHAT'S THE GLYCEMIC INDEX ALL ABOUT?

The glycemic index (GI), which was created by a group of researchers at the University of Toronto in 1981, is a list of foods that contain carbohydrates. The foods are ranked by how they affect blood sugar. Foods that appear higher on the list are digested fast and cause blood sugar to spike and rapidly drop, while slow-to-digest foods appear lower on the glycemic index because they keep blood sugar more stable, so you feel fuller. You want to eat high GI foods (with a ranking of 70 or more) sparingly and pad your diet with low (55 or less) and medium (56 to 69) ones. Steel-cut oatmeal, sweet potatoes, beans, nontropical fruits, nonstarchy veggies, and nuts rank as low. Brown rice and regular pasta fall into the medium category, and white rice, white potatoes, white bread and bagels, pretzels, and watermelon are in the high category.

"Net Carbs"—Don't Be Scammed

If you scan the label of a nutrition bar, for example, you'll see "net carbs" in the carb column. Manufacturers are doing some creative math here by subtracting grams of fiber and sugar alcohols (natural sugar substitutes) from the overall carb count, implying that these ingredients cancel out a chunk of the carbs. But it's not that clear-cut. The FDA and American Diabetes Association (ADA) do not recognize the term "net carbs," and the ADA warns that these calculations may not be accurate and may lowball how the food affects blood sugar. So until research proves that "net carbs" are legit, pay attention to the *total* amount of carbohydrates listed on a label.

THREE SQUARES OR MINI MEALS?

Grazing is good for cows, not for people. Despite the barrage of advice about eating mini meals scattered throughout the day as opposed to three larger meals, research shows that this strategy doesn't work when it comes to weight loss. A study from the *British Journal of Nutrition*[8] compared the effects of eating six times a day against eating three larger meals and found that people who ate small

HELP—EXERCISE MAKES ME SO HUNGRY!

A friend once told me she doesn't exercise because it makes her too hungry. Cue the eye-rolling. But I later realized she had a point—working out, especially at a high intensity, can burn through the carbs and fat that your body stores for energy, leaving you feeling ravenous. Research that appeared in the *American Journal of Clinical Nutrition*[9] showed that when young women worked out hard, they chowed significantly more at their next meal than women who didn't exercise—and they ate enough throughout the day to cancel out the calorie-burning benefits of their workout. To prevent eating *more* than you are torching, time your workout so you are eating a meal within an hour of wrapping up your routine (like exercising before breakfast or dinner), and make sure the meal is high in healthy carbs and protein (like peanut butter on whole grain bread or a smoothie made with fruit and almond milk), which will help restore your energy and shush those hunger pangs.

meals lost no more weight after 8 weeks than those who ate three squares. Czechoslovakian researchers[10] took the idea a step further and had people with type 2 diabetes eat just two meals (breakfast and lunch—notice they weren't suggesting anyone miss breakfast!) and another group eat six small meals, which when added together contained the same number of calories and the same nutrients as the other group's two meals. Guess what? The two-meal group lost more body fat after 12 weeks than the grazers. Of course, eating just two meals isn't going to cut it for most people, but you get the point.

The main problems are that grazing provides more opportunities to overeat, makes it harder to keep tabs on how many calories you're consuming, and causes you to think about food all day long, which isn't helpful for people who already think about food all day long. A better strategy is to sit down for three well-balanced meals and allow yourself two small *planned* snacks (calling them snacks instead of meals helps drive home the fact you're not supposed to eat too much)—one in the morning and one in the afternoon, which will keep blood sugar stable.

NAME: **Kacey Lauchnor**
AGE: **27**
HOMETOWN: **Herriman, Utah**
BEFORE WEIGHT: **232**
AFTER WEIGHT: **137**

THE MAGIC OF MINDFUL EATING

You know how you can blow through a bag of chips while watching TV without even realizing it? That's mindless eating. On the other end of the spectrum is mindful eating (also sometimes referred to as intuitive eating), which is all about eating when you are hungry, eating slowly to savor the flavor of your food, and eating whatever gives you pleasure.

SWEET NOTHINGS

I am a recovering Diet Coke-aholic. I drank it like water. Sometimes I drank it instead of water. And my colleagues used to look at me like I was freebasing heroin when I'd snap open a can. Artificial sweeteners (like aspartame, sucralose, and acesulfame potassium) may have a bad reputation, but they are considered safe by the FDA and the National Cancer Institute reports there is no evidence of an association between FDA-approved sweeteners and cancer in humans.

Still, a review of studies, published in the journal *Trends in Endocrinology & Metabolism*,[11] found that consuming artificial sweeteners—as few as one diet soda a day—is linked to an increased likelihood of weight gain. One potential reason: Sugar sub-stitutes can mess with your body's food cues. In other words, your body registers a sweet flavor and gets all excited to get some calories. Only the calories don't arrive, so it starts begging you—in the form of hunger pangs and cravings—for some calories, so you eat more. Another problem: When people drink a diet soda, they tend to eat a lot more food because they feel virtuous about having a zero-calorie drink. A study from the *Journal of the Academy of Nutrition and Dietetics* showed that on days when study participants drank sugar-free drinks, they consumed 49 percent more calories from junk foods like ice cream, cookies, and french fries.[12]

Now, that doesn't mean artificial sweeteners can't work for some people. If you are thoughtful about what you are putting in your mouth (I'm talking to you, mindful eaters!) and you don't tend to overdo it with sweets, you can probably dump a sweetener in your coffee and have a sugar-free yogurt for breakfast without any negative impact on your weight. (By the way, natural sweeteners like stevia and sugar alcohols are believed to be no better than artificial ones from a weight loss standpoint.) The bottom line: It's better for your health and your waistline to stay away from sweets altogether, but if you can't live without sweet flavor, using a few sugar subs is better than consuming large amounts of sugar—which has been clearly shown to lead to diseases like diabetes and heart disease.

Research that appeared in the journal *Appetite*[13] found that people who eat based on instinct experience less food stress and have a lower BMI than people who don't eat intui-tively. Mindful eaters aren't necessarily dieters—and losing weight requires a certain amount of restriction, at least at first—but there's a lot that can be learned from this food philosophy.

For starters, mindful eaters take their sweet time when consuming meals, which helps them relish the flavor of their food and gauge satiety. In a study from Texas Christian University,[14] normal-weight diners who ate a meal in 22 minutes consumed 88 fewer calo-ries than the normal-weight participants who chowed the same food in 9 minutes. To eat more slowly (and eat less), step away from your computer, switch off the TV, and turn over your phone. Then focus on tasting each

"I Did It!"

COURTNEY'S STORY: Courtney never paid much attention to what she ate. But when she was diagnosed with polycystic ovary syndrome at age 17, a hormone imbalance that can cause you to gain weight, all the sugary snacks she was eating started to take their toll. "Every time I stepped on the scale, I'd gained 2 or 3 pounds," she says.

NAME: **Courtney Stearns**
AGE: **30**
HOMETOWN: **Charlestown, New Hampshire**
BEFORE WEIGHT: **182**
AFTER WEIGHT: **130**

WAKE-UP CALL: Feeling unable to control her weight, Courtney became depressed. Finally, a new neighbor, who happened to be a professional boxer, invited her to his gym. Something clicked and she started training.

SUCCESS SECRETS: In addition to daily boxing workouts that included jumping rope and punching bags, Courtney fueled up on protein and veggies and started satisfying her sweet tooth with fiber-filled fruit. By her first boxing tournament in February 2010, she had shed more than 30 pounds—and she went on to drop more until she hit 130. Boxing gave Courtney a self-esteem boost that trickles into every area of her life. "I used to be afraid of talking in front of people, but now I'm confident," she says. "I know I can face anything."

bite of your food—you'll be surprised at how much faster you become satiated when you pay attention to the taste of what you're putting in your mouth. "As I started to focus on eating more slowly, I began to naturally notice when I felt like stopping," says Kacey Lauchnor, 27, of Herriman, Utah, who dropped 95 pounds.

It also helps to set the table and sit down. No need to break out your grandmother's fine china, but a study published in the *Journal of Health Psychology*[15] showed that when women ate a cereal bar while walking around, they ate five times more chocolate during a taste test that followed than women who ate the cereal bar while talking to a friend or watching TV. (Essentially, eating while chatting or watching TV is bad, but walking around is even worse.) Sitting at a table (the coffee table doesn't count!) signals to your brain that you're having a meal, while our brains conveniently forget about foods that are consumed on the go.

All foods are on the table (so to speak) in mindful eating, which cuts down on hard-to-resist cravings (we tend to crave what we can't have). Mindful eaters are able to get away with eating whatever they want because they also happen to be food snobs. For example, they probably don't eat oatmeal raisin cookies if they really prefer chocolate chip. They likely don't pluck pieces of sourdough bread out of a restaurant breadbasket if they only really like baguettes. That way, they get to eat chocolate chip cookies and pieces of baguette when they *are* available—because they didn't waste calories on things they don't care that much about.

The Shape-Up Solution

Think of diet and exercise as a power couple. They complement each other, support each other, and are more successful together than apart. While research indicates that diet may matter more than exercise when it comes to losing weight, exercise is still an important piece of the weight loss puzzle. It increases lean muscle, which can boost your metabolism; it crushes calories, giving you a little more wiggle room in your diet; and even though muscle weighs more than fat, it takes up less room, so you appear slimmer and can slip into smaller sizes of clothing.

Even more important is how powerful exercise can make you feel. There's no greater feeling than crossing the finish line of a race, RXing the WOD at CrossFit, or moving up to the front row at SoulCycle—and that sense of strength can seep into other areas of your life, making you feel like you can conquer any obstacle. If you're currently a couch potato, any type of physical activity is going to improve your health and help you drop a few pounds. But certain routines and techniques lead to more fat loss than others. Behold the four secrets to a Take It All Off physique.

1. COMBINE STRENGTH AND CARDIO

For years, cardio was synonymous with exercise. Working out meant jogging, Jazzercise class, or a Jane Fonda video. Recently, the kettlebell has swung in the other direction, and everyone is all about strength training. But to lose weight, you really need a combination of both forms of exercise. Strength training builds muscle, but you won't see the muscle unless you do enough cardio to strip away the fat that's sitting on top of it.

And while cardio is good for scorching fat and calories, you need muscle to fuel your metabolism and get fit. A study published in the *Journal of Exercise Science and Physiotherapy*[1] compared the effects of aerobic exercise, strength training, and aerobic exercise plus strength training in 120 women between the ages of 20 and 40. After 6 weeks, the aerobic group lost the most weight (about 5 pounds), the mixed group lost almost the same amount, and the strength group shed almost 1 pound. But some of the weight the aerobic group lost came from muscle. Not good. The strength group preserved lean muscle while also dropping fat, and the mixed group lost about the same amount of fat but less muscle

NAME: **Amanda Green**
AGE: **39**
HOMETOWN: **Arlington, Texas**
BEFORE WEIGHT: **165**
AFTER WEIGHT: **120**

than the aerobic group, indicating that this two-pronged approach is the way to go.

Many of our Take It All Off (TIAO) superstars started off doing cardio, which helped them improve their endurance (no more huffing and puffing while walking up the stairs or kicking the soccer ball around with the kids) and lose some weight. But then many of them hit a plateau, and incorporating strength training helped them plow through the plateau and continue to see results.

Amanda Green, 39, of Arlington, Texas, dropped 15 pounds in 2 months doing hour-long cardio DVDs, but it wasn't until she started running outside and lifting weights three times a week that she was able to ditch the last 15.

Adding weight lifting to her workout routine helped Mandy Martin of Gillette, Wyoming, shed 22 pounds in 3 months. The Take It All Off Workout is broken down into strength days and cardio days, so you get a perfect balance of both types of exercise.

2. DO HIIT

To increase fat burning, you'll be cranking out high-intensity interval training (better known as HIIT) cardio routines as part of the TIAO plan. A review of studies, published in the *Journal of Obesity,*[2] showed that HIIT may torch ab flab better than any other type of workout. In one of the studies, subjects did 8-second cycle sprints followed by 12 seconds of low-intensity cycling for a total of 20 minutes three times a week. Another group of subjects did steady-state cycling for 40 minutes three times a week. After 15 weeks, the interval group shed significantly more body

fat and abdominal fat than the steady-staters. How come? Going at near max effort turns on your body's fat-burning hormones, especially growth hormone and catecholamines, which help release fat from abdominal fat stores and dump it into the bloodstream where it's delivered to the muscles to be used up as

NAME: **Mandy Martin**
AGE: **30**
HOMETOWN: **Gillette, Wyoming**
BEFORE WEIGHT: **185**
AFTER WEIGHT: **133**

HEY, WHAT HAPPENED TO MY METABOLISM?

This is a question many women start asking themselves around the age of 40. Metabolism is the speed at which your body burns calories, and basal metabolism refers to how many calories your body burns while you are sitting around doing nothing. Basal metabolism starts dropping by about 1 to 2 percent per decade starting in your twenties (although most people don't start to notice that drop until they hit their forties). Also, we lose 8 percent of our muscle mass between the ages of 40 and 50. Since muscle burns more calories at rest than fat, the more muscle you lose, the more sluggish your basal metabolism will become. But you can easily keep your metabolism revving by strength training to increase muscle mass (see the strength moves in Chapter 9) and engaging in aerobic exercise—research in the journal *Physician and Sports-Medicine*[3] shows that doing aerobic exercise like running, biking, or swimming four to five times a week can reduce age-related muscle loss.

energy. This isn't just a cardio thing, either—fast-paced strength circuits (that often include moves like burpees, mountain climbers, speed skaters, deadlifts, and walking lunges) done with little rest between sets can set off a similar hormone reaction.

3. BE ACTIVE EVERY DAY

On the Take It All Off Plan, you will be working up a sweat 6 days a week. A study from the *Journal of Strength and Conditioning Research*[4] found that when participants were told to exercise more than four times per week for 30 minutes each time, they lost significantly more fat after 8 weeks than the study subjects instructed to work out twice a week, three or four times a week, or not at all.

The reason: Losing weight is mathematical. You need to cut enough calories per day through a combination of diet and exercise so you wind up with a calorie deficit of 3,500 by the end of the week, which results in a pound of loss. (Yeah, you could do this exclusively through your diet, but you'd be starving because you'd have to cut extra calories to make up for the lack of exercise.) Building muscle also fuels your metabolism, so you start torching more calories at rest.

What's more, exercising 6 days a week enables you to do strength and cardio on separate days so you aren't taxing the same muscles 2 days in a row and are allowing yourself enough recovery time between types of workouts, which helps prevent injury. And while it might be tempting to collapse on the couch on your day off, it's important to squeeze in a little low-impact activity. Nothing crazy—just something that's fun and relaxing like yoga, walking, gardening—even cruising around the mall. Low-impact exercise aids in muscle recovery by keeping blood flowing at optimal levels.

Burn More Fat

Supercharge your cardio-machine routine with these simple tweaks.

On the Treadmill . . .

Don't bounce. Focus on moving forward, not bounding up and down, and keep your arms close to your sides, as opposed to swinging them across your body. These form adjustments will help you run faster and more efficiently, which ups your calorie burn.

Squeeze your booty. While fast walking on the treadmill, clench your glutes as you push off with your toes to give your butt an extra workout.

Increase the resistance. To mimic the intensity and difficulty of an outdoor jog, raise the incline to 1 to 2 percent.

Recruit more muscles. To target muscles that don't usually see much action during a typical run, do the following routine at the end of your jog: Slow the speed down to 2.5 to 3.5 miles per hour. Then skip for 30 seconds, walk for 30 seconds, walk backward for 30 seconds, stand sideways and shuffle with your left foot for 30 seconds, walk for 30 seconds, and repeat with your right foot for 30 seconds.

On the Elliptical Trainer . . .

Use a light touch. Lightly rest your hands on the rails—don't white-knuckle them! Gripping the handles makes it easier for your legs to move, and you want those legs going hard!

Exercise your abs. The elliptical is primarily a lower-body machine, but you can still work your core. For example, if you're on a lower-body elliptical (not one that requires you to push and pull with your arms), hold your arms in a running position—elbows bent, upper arms close to your ribs—and contract your ab muscles as you move.

Let the music move you. Elliptical machines are tricky because speed and resistance levels vary based on the brand and model of the machine. For example, a nine might be hard on one machine and easy on another. A good way to ensure you're getting a challenging workout is to listen to music with the machine set at a moderately tough level (your legs aren't flying, but you also don't feel like you're trying to run through water), and then jack up your resistance during the chorus of every song.

On the Stationary Bike . . .

Crank it up. Every 2 or 3 minutes turn the resistance knob one full crank to mimic hill climbs.

"I Did It!"

KELLY'S STORY: Growing up, Kelly didn't reflect much on her eating habits. She'd satisfy afternoon cravings with heaps of canned frosting, and while working at a pet store, she'd polish off a 16-ounce bag of gummy bears. In her late teens, Kelly's pants size ticked up—until she had to ask her favorite clothing store to special-order size 18 jeans.

WAKE-UP CALL: It was only at age 24, when she began nursing school, that Kelly could see the impact of her 212-pound body on her long-term health. She encountered dozens of patients with obesity-induced diabetes and heart disease. She spent 2 years cycling through various diets, losing 15 pounds each time but gaining back most of it whenever she deviated from structured eating.

SUCCESS SECRETS: At 190 pounds, Kelly discovered a weight-loss blogger whose "before" body mirrored her own. She began to follow the tips and added a half-hour of cardio and weight lifting 2 or 3 days a week. Her goal: to do a fitness photo shoot by age 30. Kelly worked up to exercising 5 days a week, doing cardio and strength training on the same day 4 days a week, and high-intensity interval training 1 day a week to reach 165 pounds. She followed targeted diets to decrease fat and build muscle and focused heavily on prepping her meals ahead of time.

One week shy of her 30th birthday, Kelly reached her target weight of 150 and posed for her fitness shoot. "I've never been happier, but I want to keep improving," said Kelly. She lost 10 more pounds for her wedding, which was in May 2016 and is now focused on building more sexy muscle. "Don't be afraid to lift!" Kelly says. "You will not look like a man. I want people to know that."

| NAME: **Kelly Wasko** |
| AGE: **31** |
| HOMETOWN: **Sandy Hook, Connecticut** |
| BEFORE WEIGHT: **212** |
| AFTER WEIGHT: **140** |

Pick up the pace. Shoot for a pace of 60 to 80 revolutions per minute on hills and 80 to 110 revs on flats. Find your pace by counting how many times one foot goes around in 15 seconds and multiply that number by four.

Sit your butt down. Most of us feel the urge to stand when we're climbing "hills," but that actually makes your workout easier. When you stand, you tend to use your body weight for momentum; planting your butt on the seat forces your legs to work harder. If the resistance is so heavy that you need to stand, don't put all of your weight in the handlebars. Hover your lower body just over the seat and keep your legs bent as if you're squatting over the bike.

4. EXCUSE-PROOF YOUR WORKOUT

In order to establish an exercise habit, you need to make your workouts hard to blow off. That's why the Take It All Off Plan is designed to be done at home. When you're not feeling your fittest, it can be intimidating to step into a gym and run or walk or lift amongst spandex-clad women with perky butts. Keeping it local also gives you freedom and flexibility. You can hop on your elliptical machine while your baby naps, like Zakiee Labib. You can slip in a strength training session at 5:30 a.m., instead of having to wait for your gym to open. You probably aren't going to hightail it over to a health club to run on the treadmill for 15 minutes, but you can easily take a 15-minute jog

(continued on page 60)

GET COMPETITIVE!

There's a reason they call it healthy competition: Testing yourself can help you slip down and get fit. Within months of starting an exercise program, 10 of our TIAO superstars, also formerly sedentary women, started running races (5-Ks, half-marathons—even 26.2!), and three have become competitive triathletes. Courtney Stearns participates in boxing competitions, and Mandy Martin has seven bodybuilding competitions under her (now much smaller) belt.

Here's why you should sign up for an event today.

- Competition keeps people motivated as they strive toward a goal.
- Training groups provide a support network.
- Working out with just one other person creates accountability (you don't want to let your partner down by bailing on a training run).
- Crossing the finish line builds feelings of pride and

confidence—just what you need when you're trying to lose weight.

Road Runners Club of America (rrca.org) can help you find a running club in your area, or pop into your local running shoe store or bike shop and ask if they organize group runs or rides—most do. To find local races, log on to active.com. You can also join meetup groups to train for other events.

"I Did It!"

NAME: **Larissa Reggetto**

AGE: **25**

HOMETOWN: **Bethlehem, Pennsylvania**

BEFORE WEIGHT: **265**

AFTER WEIGHT: **160**

LARISSA'S STORY: As a kid, Larissa Reggetto could always be found on the softball field or basketball court, but that changed when her family moved from their close-knit New Jersey town to Effort, Pennsylvania, before she started high school. "I didn't want to be there, so I didn't try to make friends," says Larissa. She quit sports and filled her time with fast-food runs. As a senior, Larissa, 5 feet 5 inches, weighed 265 pounds.

WAKE-UP CALL: During college, Larissa studied criminal justice and dreamed of becoming a police officer. As she neared graduation, she checked the fitness requirements for the police academy, and her heart sank. "I realized I was nowhere near where I needed to be. I had to change, or else I wouldn't make it," she says.

SUCCESS SECRETS: Larissa replaced big, greasy binges with six to eight small meals a day. In 2 weeks she lost 10 pounds, a confidence-boosting drop that got Larissa back in the gym. A trainer helped her add cycling, weight lifting, and circuit training into her routine five times a week, and in 10 months she'd reached 185 pounds.

When Larissa took her workouts onto new terrain outside, she clicked into another gear and hit 152 pounds by February 2013. That same month, she passed (okay, destroyed) the police-academy fitness exam. As a police cadet, Larissa learned defensive tactics that she says would have been impossible at her old weight. Now at a healthy 160 pounds, she can run 10 miles and bust out 50 pushups on cue, and she is the go-to girl for fitness plans at the police station. "But the mental aspect is the biggest change," she says. "I used to be shy. As a police officer, you need confidence and courage. I finally have what it takes."

Her advice for people tackling their own weight loss journey? "There's no goal ever too big," she says. "You have to get over the fear of the transformation and from there you'll see extreme progress. Have no fear at all."

around the block. "I got an exercise bike so I can work out whenever I want. I like to pedal while I watch TV," says Sarah DeArmond, 30, of Calera, Alabama, who dropped 100 pounds. Bridget Rauschenberg runs the stairs of her apartment building.

But sweating solo isn't for everyone. Some people need structure and social support and find meeting a trainer at the gym or a friend at the park prevents them from bailing on workouts. Here are some other motivational tips to help you stay on track.

- "I update a vision board every month with motivational quotes and pictures from magazines. It helps me stay focused on my dreams."—Leanna Reiling

- "Pay for [fitness] classes in advance—you won't skip them."—Alexandra Shipper

- "Every 10 pounds I lost, I posted a little 'Woo-hoo me!' on Facebook. It keeps you pumped."—Katie Russell

- "Set [your gear] out the night before: clothes, weights, water bottle. Then nothing can get in the way of your workout." —Krystal Sanders

- "I always listen to music while I run. Try something with a strong, quick beat."—Jen Punda

- "Knowing I had to post my weight [on the blog I created to chronicle my weight loss] each Monday was an incredible motivator."—Hannah Casey

NAME: **Leanna Reiling**
AGE: **35**
HOMETOWN: **Beaverton, Oregon**
BEFORE WEIGHT: **256**
AFTER WEIGHT: **149**

- This one is from me: Whenever you're feeling unmotivated, mentally commit to doing just half of your workout. In most cases, once you get started you'll be inspired to keep going!

6

5-Day Quick Start

Think of the Take It All Off Quick Start as a prep course. The goal is to introduce you to a variety of nutritious ingredients while temporarily eliminating things that may be causing you to gain weight—or feel bloated, sick, or lethargic. You will be enjoying real food (no weird juices), and you don't need to worry about counting calories or measuring portions right now. The Quick Start only lasts for 5 days; then you'll move on to the Take It All Off Plan, which will allow you to add back most foods in moderation.

But maybe you'll realize you don't even miss them. Maybe you'll notice you feel so much better without them. It's like being on a "break" in a relationship—you need some time away from a food to figure out if you truly love it and can't live without it. Sometimes giving yourself space makes you realize you have feelings for something else.

NAME: **Melanie Kitchen**

AGE: **41**

HOMETOWN: **Grand Island, New York**

BEFORE WEIGHT: **190**

AFTER WEIGHT: **125**

"Once I got rid of junk, I found I liked fruits and vegetables," says Melanie Kitchen of Grand Island, New York, who lost 65 pounds thanks to healthier eating habits.

FOR THIS QUICK START PLAN . . .

You'll be eating three meals and two snacks every day. As I mentioned before, you don't have to worry too much about portions and calories here because the focus is on getting used to eating healthy foods and eliminating foods that can cause bloating, weight gain, lethargy, and possible food intolerances. Once you know which foods work for you and which don't, you'll move on to the diet, where you'll start counting calories and practicing portion control. We'll begin with a sample meal plan, and then give you some basic Quick Start guidelines (foods to avoid, foods to eat) so you can create your own meals, too.

Sample Meal Plan for the 5-Day Quick Start

DAY 1

BREAKFAST	SNACK	LUNCH	SNACK	DINNER
⅓ cup (dry) steel-cut oatmeal, cooked, with fresh blueberries + 2 eggs, scrambled	Chocolate-Cherry Bliss protein smoothie (page 133)	2 slices sprouted grain bread (Ezekiel 4:9) with 4 ounces sliced chicken breast + deli mustard, lettuce, and sliced tomato	Celery sticks with 2 tablespoons hemp seed butter	Pork Tenderloin with Butternut Squash and Steamed Spinach (page 107)

DAY 2

BREAKFAST	SNACK	LUNCH	SNACK	DINNER
1 slice sprouted grain bread (Ezekiel 4:9), toasted, topped with 2 tablespoons natural peanut butter, eaten with fresh strawberries	Handful of walnuts + 1 cup blackberries	Mixed greens with veggies of choice + 1 can water-packed light tuna (drained) + black olives + white wine vinegar or balsamic vinegar	½ cup steamed edamame	4-ounce turkey breast cutlet + ½ cup cooked brown rice + steamed broccoli

DAY 3

BREAKFAST	SNACK	LUNCH	SNACK	DINNER
Scrambled Veggie Eggs (page 82)	Vanilla Pumpkin Pie protein smoothie (page 133)	Lightened-Up Chicken Salad (page 94)	Banana-Walnut Protein Bar (page 126)	Spaghetti Squash with Turkey Tomato Sauce (page 106)

DAY 4

BREAKFAST	SNACK	LUNCH	SNACK	DINNER
Avocado Toast with Fried Eggs (page 89)	Peanut Butter–Flax Fudge Bar (page 127)	Spaghetti Squash with Turkey Tomato Sauce (leftovers from last night's dinner)	Baby carrots with 2 tablespoons hemp seed butter	Seafood Rice (page 116) with Mixed Greens Salad (page 92)

DAY 5

BREAKFAST	SNACK	LUNCH	SNACK	DINNER
Veggie-Stuffed Cheese Omelet (omit the cheese; page 84)	Handful of walnuts + 1 cup strawberries	Sprouted Grain Tuna Sandwich (page 95)	Apple Pie in a Cup protein smoothie (page 135)	Beef and Kale Stir-Fry (page 108)

FOODS TO AVOID FOR THE NEXT 5 DAYS

These eats can cause bloating, constipation, indigestion, and gassiness—which can make you feel sick and look heavier than you really are. Plus, most don't contain nutrients essential for health and weight loss. So don't eat them!

Anything made with wheat flour (pasta, bread, bagels, wraps, muffins, pretzels, crackers, granola bars—you get the picture). Wheat flour has little significant nutritional value and can cause digestive issues for some people (think gluten). Plus, foods made with it often contain preservatives and sugar.

"I Did It!"

NAME: **Jennifer Sierra**
AGE: **31**
HOMETOWN: **Houston, Texas**
BEFORE WEIGHT: **183**
AFTER WEIGHT: **118**

JENNIFER'S STORY: Jennifer was 13 when her mother first put her on a diet. Among five siblings, "I was always the heaviest," she says. Jennifer, who stands just under 5 feet 3 inches, yo-yoed between 140 and 160 pounds until her marriage at age 21, when things fell apart without Mom's hovering eye. "I'd eat greasy sandwiches for breakfast and lunch, then anything fried for dinner," says Jennifer. In 2009, having a baby left her at a peak of over 180 pounds.

WAKE-UP CALL: Jennifer, whose pregnancy weight stayed put, avoided reality for about a year, until late 2010, when she spied an unflattering Facebook pic: "I honestly didn't recognize myself," she says. Jennifer admitted she needed a kick in the butt and signed on with a trainer in May 2012.

SUCCESS SECRETS: Jennifer confronted her gym phobia and met with her trainer for Saturday sessions of pushups, squats, presses, and lunges. On other days, she put in 30 minutes of a

cardio-boosting walk-run combo on the treadmill. She also started planning and packing her meals in advance, with an eye on protein, carbs, and fat instead of just calories. By fall of 2012, Jennifer was down to about 145 pounds. To reach the next level, she upped her tough workouts to four times per week, targeting a different muscle group each day. By May 2013, Jennifer, who could now easily don a size zero, weighed under 120 pounds. In 2015, while training for her first bodybuilding competition, Jennifer became pregnant with her second child. After giving birth then losing the weight a second time(!), she flaunted her toned body in a bodybuilding competition.

Alcohol. It doesn't necessarily make you fat (more on that later), but drinking can hijack your willpower and make you feel bloated. So lay off it for now.

Dairy products made from cow's milk. They contain hormones that can have adverse effects on your health, and lactose (an ingredient in milk) can cause digestive problems and skin issues. And while protein-rich dairy products can have a place in a weight loss program—organic versions get the green light in the Take It All Off Eating Plan—some dieters tend to go overboard with them (milk in their morning cereal, yogurt for a snack, cheese in their lunch salad, and so on), which doesn't leave room for other protein-rich foods and may cause your body to develop a dairy intolerance. To ditch dairy dependence, avoid it for the next 5 days.

Cured deli meats, which contain sodium nitrite, a chemical that has been linked to cancer.

Artificial sweeteners. As you know from Chapter 4, sugar substitutes can cause serious sugar cravings and lead to overeating. Cutting them out during the Quick Start may help you kick (or at least control) your sweet tooth.

Meal replacement bars. Some bars are healthy—and are worthy stand-ins for meals when you're on the go—especially

NAME: **Ashley Nunn**
AGE: **35**
HOMETOWN: **Charleston, West Virginia**
BEFORE WEIGHT: **264**
CURRENT WEIGHT: **144**

those that do not contain soy protein isolate. But this Quick Start is all about whole, unprocessed foods, so avoid them for now.

EAT CLEANER, FEEL BETTER

There's been a lot of buzz lately about clean eating, which basically just means eating more whole foods (fruit, veggies, whole grains, nuts, seeds, and plant- and animal-based proteins) and fewer processed ones. It's a legit concept, with some undeniable perks. Whole foods are less likely to contain sketchy chemicals and usually contain fewer calories than processed foods. Five months of clean eating helped Mandy Martin trim down by 20 pounds.

It can even boost your mood, according to a recent study in the *British Journal of Health Psychology*.[1] The researchers discovered that eating more fruits and veggies was associated with happiness, curiosity, creativity, and life satisfaction. Is it the nutrients in the produce that improve our disposition and clear our mind? Could be. Or is it that replacing sugary snacks with fiber-filled whole fruit helps us dodge blood sugar crashes that make us testy? Maybe. Or is it purely psychosomatic? In other words, you feel better because you're eating foods that are supposed to make you feel better. Ultimately, who cares? All that matters is that you feel good.

That said, you don't necessarily have to banish all packaged foods—they can be a boon to dieters because serving size, calories, fat, and carbs are clearly labeled on the ingredient list, making it easer to keep tabs on what—and how much—one is consuming. The best option is to choose packaged foods with short ingredient lists (fewer than eight items) consisting of ingredients that you have actually heard of.

"I try to eat foods that have no more than three ingredients, so what I am putting in my mouth is as natural as possible," says Katrina McCloud.

Soda (both diet and regular), candy, baked goods, ice cream, and all fried foods. No explanation needed.

Canned or dried fruit, which can contain nearly as much sugar as a bag of Skittles, should be avoided.

Beans. Unlike most of the other foods on this list, beans are nutrient-packed and deserve a starring role in your diet. But they are banned during the Quick Start because they cause gas and bloating. (Bloating can make you look about 3 months pregnant and cause you to retain water, making the needle on the scale go up.)

Beat Belly Bloat

Bloat, which is triggered by water retention or gas, isn't fat—but it can give you a gut. Keep your abs looking flat by laying off notorious bloaters like salt and booze and by limiting foods that contain FODMAPs—fermentable oligosaccharides, disaccharides, monosaccharides, and polyols. FODMAPs are food molecules that are normally absorbed in the small

DO YOU HAVE A DRINKING PROBLEM?

Every day your body loses water when you pee and sweat—even breathing causes you to excrete agua! So if you don't drink enough H_2O, you put yourself at risk for dehydration, which can trigger headaches, exhaustion, and other health issues. What's more, researchers at the University of Connecticut[2] found that women who drink the recommended amount of water (which is eight 8-ounce glasses per day) tend to be in a better mood and are less prone to tension, depression, and confusion. While the recommendation is eight 8-ounce glasses, many experts believe this number needs to be bumped up to more like 10 glasses per day. And if it's super hot out or you sweat like crazy when you exercise, you'll need to pour yourself an extra 8-ounce glass per day (on top of the 10 you should be drinking).

intestine of the digestive tract. Some people have trouble absorbing FODMAPs, and the unabsorbed FODMAPs land in the large intestine where they ferment and cause abdominal pain, gas, nausea, constipation, and/or diarrhea. Here is a list of common FODMAP foods.

- Almonds
- Apples
- Artichokes
- Avocado
- Beans
- Brussels sprouts
- Cabbage
- Cashews
- Cauliflower
- Dairy
- Garlic
- Mushrooms
- Onions
- Pears
- Sweeteners (artificial ones and sugar alcohols)
- Wheat (only some people are affected by wheat)

FOODS TO EAT FOR THE NEXT 5 DAYS

Add these Quick Start staples to your shopping cart.

- Veggies like lettuce, celery, cucumbers, carrots, tomatoes, green beans, broccoli, squash, kale, spinach, sweet potatoes, and bell peppers. Aim to eat five types of vegetables per day to ensure you're getting a variety of important nutrients and antioxidants.

- Fruits like berries, apples, oranges, nectarines, pears, melon, and peaches. Shoot for one to three servings a day.

- Unprocessed lean animal proteins like eggs, chicken, turkey, beef, bison, pork, lamb, fish, and shellfish. Look for words like "free range" or "grass fed" when selecting meat and poultry, and "wild" when shopping for fish. Will the regular stuff kill you or make you gain weight? No. But if you can find and afford them, these types of protein are believed to be slightly healthier.

- Healthy fats, which include nuts, seeds, natural nut and seed butters (peanut, almond, hemp), hummus, olive oil, and coconut oil.

- Whole grains like brown rice, barley, quinoa, teff, oats, freekeh, and sprouted grain bread.

- Seltzer and tea. When plain old water just won't cut it, drink calorie-free, naturally flavored seltzer, which can satisfy a soda craving–and the carbonation makes you feel full. Hot tea, unsweetened iced tea, and coffee are also on the table—provided you don't dump in sugar, artificial sweeteners, or cow's milk.

When to Buy Organic

Eating organic isn't going to make you slimmer, but it might make you healthier, because certified organic foods are made without pesticides, preservatives, and hormones, which *may* lead to a variety of ailments. And organic foods definitely have more flavor. A lot of products pitch themselves as organic, but to make sure you're getting the real deal, look for the green-and-white "USDA Organic" seal on the packaging. When shopping for loose produce, check the sticker. Each sticker has a code; the code on organic produce starts with a 9. If you can't afford to buy all organic foods, at least make sure to go au naturel on the Environmental Working Group's "Dirty Dozen"—a list of 12 fruits and veggies that tend to be high in pesticides that can't be rinsed off. Here are the offenders.

- Apples
- Bell peppers
- Celery
- Cherries
- Cherry tomatoes
- Cucumbers
- Grapes
- Nectarines
- Peaches
- Spinach
- Strawberries
- Tomatoes

"I Did It!"

DJ'S STORY: DJ was an emotional eater. Crushed by the pressure of running a daycare business and working weekends as a nurse's aide—not to mention being the mother of four kids—she would soothe herself with fattening foods. The comfort food, plus her mostly sedentary lifestyle, left DJ, 5 feet 3 inches, weighing in at 240 pounds.

NAME: **DJ Gray**

AGE: **37**

HOMETOWN: **Lilly, Pennsylvania**

BEFORE WEIGHT: **240**

AFTER WEIGHT: **125**

WAKE-UP CALL: In October 2012, DJ discovered a lump in her breast and feared she had breast cancer, which runs in her family. Her tests came back negative, but the scare prompted her to take a hard look at her health. "The doctor said the mass could be due to my weight gain," she says. "I knew if I wanted to be around for a long time, I needed to change things."

SUCCESS SECRETS: DJ bought a food scale to help her prepare portion-controlled meals. "I used to eat three bowls of granola at a time," she says. "Now I know what's a healthy amount." She gradually weeded out fried foods, sugary cereals, and extra desserts from her diet. "My biggest dietary change was saying no to all of the kids' leftovers," she says. Now, her whole system is rewired: The last time she had a chicken nugget, she spit it right back out! "It doesn't even taste good anymore," she says. In addition to doing at-home exercise DVDs, DJ started running the length of her street, 1.2 miles, every other day, which helped her to drop the last 70 pounds. Now she runs multiple 5-Ks a year—and almost always places in the top three of her age group. "I never believed I'd be able to do this much," she says.

The TIAO
Eating Plan

You've already come a long way. You've figured out how many pounds you need to drop, mastered healthy eating habits, honed your willpower, and learned which foods trigger weight loss. And you've probably gained some helpful insights as to why you gained the weight in the first place. Now it's time to start losing it—by paring down portions, keeping track of your calories, and building your meals around filling, muscle-building protein.

After finishing the Quick Start, most foods are back in play, if you decide you want to revisit them. You can now have organic dairy products, provided they don't mess with your stomach. Bloating foods like beans, apples, pears, onion, garlic, mushrooms, avocado, cabbage, raw broccoli, cauliflower, Brussels sprouts, and almonds are welcome, but add them back in one at a time and wait 48 hours before introducing the next one. (Whip out your food journal and record how you feel after each meal and snack to zero in on which foods make you bloated. Using

RAISING THE BAR

As you know from Chapter 2, my favorite nutrition bars are the NuGo Slim Raspberry Truffle and the Dark Chocolate, Nuts & Sea Salt KIND bar, which somehow manage to taste like candy while being high in protein and other nutrients and super low in sugar. When choosing a bar, make sure it's all-natural and contains 100 to 250 calories if you're planning to eat it as a snack (you can go up to 450 calories if you're having it as a meal). Also make sure that it has a minimum of 4 grams of protein (and no more than 40 grams), no more than 50 grams of carbohydrates, and no more than 30 grams of fat. Here are some other bars that fit the bill.

- fücoPROTEIN by Garden of Life
- Greens+ Protein Bar (whey protein) and Greens+ Plusbar Whey Crisp
- Honey Stinger Protein Bar
- LÄRABAR
- Organic Food Bar (choose Active Greens or Protein variety)
- Organic Green Super Food
- Perfect Food Bar by Garden of Life
- Perfect Weight America Bar by Garden of Life
- PranaBar
- Pure bars
- Think Fruit
- Vega Whole Food Energy Bar
- Zero Impact bars by VPX

an app like mySymptoms can also help track pesky and persistent food-related problems.) And you can now sprinkle natural nutrition bars into your diet, which are great when you're on the go (see "Raising the Bar").

A few things are still off-limits—including fried foods; processed meats, like bacon, hot dogs, and sausage; dried fruit that contains added sugar (I'm looking at you, Craisins); soda (diet or regular); anything made with wheat flour; anything that contains artificial sweeteners; snack foods like chips and pretzels; candy; desserts like ice cream and baked goods; and alcohol. You get one freebie per week—so if you want a glass of wine on Saturday night or an order of french fries one day for lunch, go ahead! Just keep in mind that any more than one splurge per week could prevent you from seeing results. You should stay on the Take It All Off Eating Plan for at least 8 weeks—or until you've hit your goal weight—and you can expect to lose 1 or 2 pounds per week.

THE RULES

Like in the Quick Start, you will be eating five times per day—three meals and two snacks. Your meals and snacks should be spaced 2 to 5 hours apart. As I've mentioned in this book, breakfast can promote weight

"*I Did It!*"

KIM'S STORY: Unlike most of the women in this book, Kim was thin as a teenager. Her metabolism was so speedy that her body bounced right back after having her first baby at age 21. But she eventually started gaining weight thanks to greasy takeout and frequent restaurant meals with her now husband—and all of the fad diets she tried backfired.

NAME: **Kim Schoenfeldt**
AGE: **42**
HOMETOWN: **Miami, Florida**
BEFORE WEIGHT: **225**
AFTER WEIGHT: **122**

WAKE-UP CALL: On a trip to Disney World in December 2009, Kim was mortified when she couldn't wedge through the park's turnstile. "I tried to forget it," Kim says. And she did, for a year—until her husband was diagnosed with diabetes, and she realized she needed to change her habits, too.

SUCCESS SECRETS: Kim began by eating smaller portions. "I used to have a whole basket of rolls at dinner," she says. "But I learned to stop at one." At home her husband made new versions of their old go-tos, like flatbread pizzas with veggies and low-fat cheese, instead of ordering delivery. In 3 months, Kim lost 22 pounds. She did exercise DVDs 3 or 4 days a week and now does a combo of cardio, strength training, and stretching. Kim reached her goal weight of 128 pounds on March 12, 2012, and has since whittled off a few more bonus pounds to settle at 122.

loss. But if you're antibreakfast, you can have black coffee (with a dash of cream) or nothing at all—and kick off your day with the midmorning snack.

Each meal or snack must contain the following three items.

- A low-fat, natural form of protein from either an animal source (eggs, fish, meat, pork, poultry, cheese, yogurt, milk) or a plant source (nuts, nut butters, beans). Aim for at least 15 grams per meal and at least 6 grams per snack.

- A whole veggie or fruit. Eat at least one serving of veggies at three of your meals and snacks; if you choose, you can have a fruit instead of a veggie at your other two. Eat nonstarchy vegetables, like broccoli, asparagus, squash, bell peppers, tomatoes, artichokes, cabbage, carrots, cauliflower, celery, cucumbers, eggplant, kale, lettuce, onions, radishes, spinach, Brussels sprouts, bok choy, green beans, and zucchini. Save the occasional starchy veggie—like potatoes, peas, turnips, and corn—for after a workout, when your body is at its calorie-burning peak.

- A hydrating beverage.
  - Water (can contain lemon)
  - Seltzer
  - Tea (herbal or green are best)*
  - Coffee (a dash of cream is okay, but no sugar or sweetener)*

- Unsweetened almond or coconut milk
- Organic cow's milk

  * *Coffee, tea, and other caffeinated beverages are not dehydrating, shows research from the University of Connecticut.*[1]

Optional Items

- Small amounts of "good" fats—such as avocado, olive oil, butter, flax oil, coconut oil, fish oil, or olives—are encouraged at every meal but not required. Use oils and nut butters and solid foods like nuts.

- Whole grains are full of health benefits, and some contain a little protein, but they tend to have more calories than lean animal proteins and veggies. Try oats, brown rice, teff, quinoa, freekeh, barley, bulgur, and buckwheat. You can also have low-sugar cereals—such as All-Bran Buds, Bran Flakes, Cheerios, Ezekiel 4:9 cereals (all flavors), and Shredded Wheat—and crackers, like GG Bran Crispbread, Wasa Fiber Crispbread, Ryvita Crispbread, rice crackers, and even original flavor Triscuits! For bread, go with a sprouted grain bread, like Ezekiel 4:9. And in place of pasta, try shirataki noodles—a gluten-free Asian noodle made from konjac yams, which contain only 10 (seriously, 10!) calories per serving and are super low in carbs (around 3 grams per 4-ounce serving)—or spaghetti squash.

FIVE FLAT-BELLY FOODS

RESEARCH SHOWS THESE EATS CAN HELP SLIM YOUR STOMACH.

1. Yogurt

At the University of Tennessee, Knoxville,[2] two groups of obese subjects were put on calorie-restricted diets for 12 weeks. One group ate three 6-ounce servings of yogurt a day. The yogurt group lost significantly more belly fat than the other dieters, possibly because dairy products are able to suppress a type of hormone associated with abdominal fat storage. The study participants were eating regular fat-free yogurt, but opt for 0% Greek instead, which contains more protein.

2. Eggs

Research that appeared in the *International Journal of Obesity*[3] showed that people on reduced-calorie diets who ate two eggs for breakfast 5 days a week lost more belly fat after 8 weeks than dieters who ate a bagel for breakfast (which contained the same number of calories as the eggs). One potential explanation: Protein-rich eggs are satiating, making you less likely to snack and overeat at meals throughout the rest of the day.

3. Whole grains

Eating whole grains *in addition* to refined white ones isn't going to help your cause, but eating them *instead* of refined carbs can help tighten your belt. A study from the *American Journal of Clinical Nutrition*[4] showed that people who eat more than three servings a day of whole grains (stuff like oatmeal, brown rice, and quinoa) tend to have 10 percent less ab flab than people who eat less than half a serving a day. The researchers aren't exactly sure why, but it may have to do with the fiber, which increases satiety and triggers hormones that prevent belly-fat storage. Remember to stick to half-cup servings and aim to eat whole grains after a workout, when your body is primed to burn carbs.

4. Chia seeds

Chias contain a type of essential fatty acid that shuttles fat away from your organs, which conveniently happen to be located in your abdominal region. So when Australian researchers[5] put rats on a high-fat, high-carb diet for 16 weeks and gave half of the test group chia seeds for the last 8 weeks of the study, the chia group lost more belly fat than the control group. Toss chias in smoothies or mix them into yogurt or oatmeal. See the Strawberry-Chia Yogurt recipe on page 124.

5. Dark chocolate

Wait, chocolate? In a book about weight loss? You got it—research[6] shows that dark chocolate is associated with lower amounts of abdominal fat. Here's one possible explanation: Seventy percent cacao dark chocolate contains a type of flavonoid that has a positive effect on insulin and cortisol levels. Have an ounce of the bittersweet treat after dinner to satisfy dessert cravings.

What to Eat Post-Workout

It's important to eat a snack or meal that contains both a complete protein (which means it has all nine essential amino acids) and a carb within an hour of exercising (this post-workout meal/snack counts as one of your five total per day). The protein will help build and repair muscle, while the carbs will replenish glycogen (carbs stored in muscle) that you drained during your workout. Smart post-workout complete-protein choices include whey protein, pea protein, hemp protein, fish, meat, eggs, poultry, and cottage cheese. Ideal carbs include brown rice, quinoa, Cheerios or other whole grain cereals, sprouted bread, potatoes (white or sweet), carrots, corn, apples, bananas, mangos, grapes, pineapple, peaches, and plums.

Calorie Calculator

To figure out how many calories you should consume each day, multiply your weight by 12 and then subtract 500. That's how many calories you should shoot for. For the days you're working out, which will be six times a week following our plan, multiply your weight by 15 instead of 12.

YOU CHEATED—SO NOW WHAT?

SLIPUPS HAPPEN. HERE'S HOW TO COURSE-CORRECT.

Cheating on your boyfriend can put an end to your relationship, but cheating on your diet doesn't have to put an end to your weight loss goal. There are planned cheats and unplanned ones. Let's talk about the planned ones first. These are special-occasion indulgences, like a slice of cake on your birthday or a plate of Bolognese chased with a dish of gelato on a trip to Italy (when in Rome . . .).

Planned diet divergences are no biggie because you probably allotted for them (meaning you worked out a little harder at the gym that day or had a smaller lunch) and you registered the food as a treat, something you don't get every day.

Unplanned cheats are a slippery slope. One cheat can suddenly snowball into a whole day (or week) of off-the-wagon eating until you've blown your diet in a hard-to-recover-from way. Here's the secret: Accept the fact you cheated, and don't beat yourself up about it. Remind yourself that because you've been eating a healthy diet and working out diligently, you probably can afford this one indiscretion—it's not going to unravel all of your hard work. Make sure your next meal is a healthy one, which will help get you right back on track.

THE PLAN

Here are 5 days' worth of menus to get you started. Recipes for most of the meals and snacks appear in the next chapter. Feel free to sub in different Take It All Off recipes or make up your own meals using the nutrition guidelines and approved foods outlined in this chapter. These daily menus ring in at around 1,350 to 1,530 calories per day; you may need to adjust the total number of calories based on your weight (see the "Calorie Calculator" section opposite).

DAY 1

BREAKFAST	SNACK	LUNCH	SNACK	DINNER
Scrambled Veggie Eggs (page 82)	Peanut Butter–Flax Fudge Bar (page 127)	Sprouted Grain Tuna Sandwich (page 95)	Mini "pizzas" (page 129)	Pork Tenderloin with Butternut Squash and Steamed Spinach (page 107)
263 calories, 23 g protein, 20 g carbohydrates, 4 g fiber, 1 g sugar, 10 g fat, 5.5 g saturated fat, 574 mg sodium	300 calories, 31 g protein, 10 g carbohydrates, 6 g fiber, 1.5 g sugar, 16 g fat, 2 g saturated fat, 121 mg sodium	331 calories, 25 g protein, 31 g carbohydrates, 6 g fiber, 3 g sugar, 11 g fat, 2 g saturated fat, 453 mg sodium	247 calories, 16 g protein, 32 g carbohydrates, 6 g fiber, 1 g sugar, 7 g fat, 3.5 g saturated fat, 392 mg sodium	213 calories, 26 g protein, 21 g carbohydrates, 5 g fiber, 3 g sugar, 4 g fat, 1 g saturated fat, 267 mg sodium

TOTAL CALORIES: 1,354
TOTAL PROTEIN: 137 GRAMS

DAY 2

BREAKFAST	SNACK	LUNCH	SNACK	DINNER
Breakfast Muffin Parfait (page 83)	Strawberry–Chia Yogurt (page 124)	Greek Lentil Soup (page 93) with Mixed Greens Salad	Banana–Walnut Protein Bar (page 126) or a packaged bar listed in "Raising the Bar" (page 72) + 1 cup unsweetened almond milk	Salmon with Sautéed Tomatoes and Quinoa (page 110)
326 calories, 24 g protein, 21 g carbohydrates, 6 g fiber, 12 g sugar, 17 g fat, 5 g saturated fat, 533 mg sodium	235 calories, 27 g protein, 18 g carbohydrates, 3 g fiber, 14 g sugar, 6 g fat, 4 g saturated fat, 82 mg sodium	301 calories, 19 g protein, 44 g carbohydrates, 16 g fiber, 14 g sugar, 6 g fat, 1 g saturated fat, 604 mg sodium	238 calories, 13 g protein, 13 g carbohydrates, 3 g fiber, 4 g sugar, 16 g fat, 2 g saturated fat, 232 mg sodium	459 calories, 31 g protein, 33 g carbohydrates, 5 g fiber, 6 g sugar, 23 g fat, 4.5 g saturated fat, 368 mg sodium

TOTAL CALORIES: 1,597
TOTAL PROTEIN: 116 GRAMS

DAY 3

BREAKFAST	SNACK	LUNCH	SNACK	DINNER
Veggie-Stuffed Cheese Omelet (page 84)	⅓ cup shelled pistachios + ½ cup fresh raspberries	Spaghetti Squash with Turkey Tomato Sauce (page 106)	Apple and Peanut Butter Dippers (page 125)	Zesty Chicken with Asparagus and Sweet Potato (page 111)
317 calories, 17 g protein, 27 g carbohydrates, 5 g fiber, 20 g sugar, 17 g fat, 5 g saturated fat, 373 mg sodium	256 calories, 9 g protein, 21 g carbohydrates, 8 g fiber, 7 g sugar, 18 g fat, 211 mg sodium	360 calories, 33 g protein, 41 g carbohydrates, 8 g fiber, 19 g sugar, 10 g fat, 3 g saturated fat, 511 mg sodium	263 calories, 9 g protein, 19 g carbohydrates, 8 g fiber, 6 g sugar, 19 g fat, 2 g saturated fat, 176 mg sodium	310 calories, 27 g protein, 15 g carbohydrates, 3 g fiber, 5 g sugar, 16 g fat, 4.5 g saturated fat, 844 mg sodium

TOTAL CALORIES: 1,506
TOTAL PROTEIN: 95 GRAMS

DAY 4

BREAKFAST	SNACK	LUNCH	SNACK	DINNER
Protein "Muesli" (page 85)	3 hard-cooked eggs + 1 clementine	Mixed Greens Salad (page 92) with 4 ounces cooked chicken breast	2 sticks light mozzarella string cheese + 1 red bell pepper cut into strips	Bison Burger (page 112) with steamed broccoli
337 calories, 22 g protein, 38 g carbohydrates, 4 g fiber, 16 g sugar, 12 g fat, 3 g saturated fat, 60 mg sodium	267 calories, 20 g protein, 11 g carbohydrates, 1 g fiber, 8 g sugar, 16 g fat, 5 g saturated fat, 187 mg sodium	225 calories, 38 g protein, 7 g carbohydrates, 3 g fiber, 4 g sugar, 4 g fat, 1 g saturated fat, 182 mg sodium	197 calories, 17 g protein, 9 g carbohydrates, 2 g fiber, 4 g sugar, 4 g fat, 1 g saturated fat, 182 mg sodium	436 calories, 32 g protein, 29 g carbohydrates, 7 g fiber, 1 g sugar, 22 g fat, 9 g saturated fat, 263 mg sodium

TOTAL CALORIES: 1,462
TOTAL PROTEIN: 129 GRAMS

DAY 5

BREAKFAST	SNACK	LUNCH	SNACK	DINNER
Overnight Steel-Cut Oats and Blueberries (page 86)	Hummus and Veggies (page 123)	Black-Eyed Pea Egg Salad (page 96) + 1 plum	High-Fiber Berry Yogurt (page 130)	Fish Tacos with Mango Salsa (page 113)
338 calories, 16 g protein, 39 g carbohydrates, 5 g fiber, 6 g sugar, 15 g fat, 1.5 g saturated fat, 155 mg sodium	174 calories, 6 g protein, 13 g carbohydrates, 4 g fiber, 2 g sugar, 12 g fat, 1.5 g saturated fat, 356 mg sodium	382 calories, 25 g protein, 32 g carbohydrates, 9 g fiber, 12 g sugar, 18 g fat, 8 g saturated fat, 606 mg sodium	260 calories, 21 g protein, 38 g carbohydrates, 5 g fiber, 10 g sugar, 4 g fat, 2 g saturated fat, 183 mg sodium	362 calories, 24 g protein, 36 g carbohydrates, 6 g fiber, 13 g sugar, 15 g fat, 2 g saturated fat, 203 mg sodium

TOTAL CALORIES: 1,516
TOTAL PROTEIN: 92 GRAMS

"I Did It!"

JESSIE'S STORY: Jessie quit smoking at age 19 and replaced cigs with another unhealthy habit: gorging on fried food and pizza. "Without cigarettes, I needed some other source of satisfaction, and I got that from richer foods," she says. Plus, a new desk job as a paralegal had her sitting on her butt all day and left her exhausted at night. "I was so beat when I got home that I didn't think much about what I ate," Jessie says.

WAKE-UP CALL: Jessie became so depressed about her size that she stopped riding her mountain bike because she no longer felt confident. In early 2012, she overheard a friend talking about calories and nutrients and decided it was high time she started paying attention to what she put in her mouth.

SUCCESS SECRETS: Jessie started trimming her portions by downloading a calorie-counting app, and she replaced her usual high-fat meals with poultry, fish, and greens. She hopped back on the elliptical machine that had been gathering dust in her home office and started pedaling for 30 minutes 5 days a week. By March 2013, she was mountain biking again and working out on the elliptical for 45 minutes each time, conquering tough interval routines. She then upped the ante by adding half-hour strength training sessions to her schedule and banging out 3-mile runs. Now she's fit, happy, and down to 115 pounds!

NAME: **Jessie Foss**
AGE: **38**
HOMETOWN: **Garland, Texas**
BEFORE WEIGHT: **215**
AFTER WEIGHT: **115**

8

The TIAO Meal Plan Recipes

You now know that cooking at home is the key to slashing calories and trimming portions. These protein-packed, fat-fighting meals will help you lose weight without sacrificing flavor or pleasure. And here's the best part: You can whip most of them up in under 30 minutes, and you don't need any cooking chops beyond the ability to read directions. Mix and match these breakfasts, lunches, dinners, and snacks to create your own nutritious and delicious meal plan. Bon appétit!

Scrambled Veggie Eggs

Salsa gives eggs Florentine a (nearly) calorie-free kick. Look for a sprouted grain bread, such as Ezekiel 4:9, in the freezer section of your grocery store.

Makes 1 serving

1 teaspoon coconut oil

½ cup liquid egg whites (or 4 egg whites)

1 egg

⅓ cup baby spinach

2 tablespoons salsa

1 slice sprouted grain bread, toasted

1. In a medium nonstick skillet over medium-high heat, melt the oil. Cook the egg whites, egg, and spinach, stirring, for 4 minutes, or until the egg is cooked to your liking and the spinach is wilted.

2. Top with the salsa and serve with the toast.

Nutrition per serving: 263 calories, 23 g protein, 20 g carbohydrates, 4 g fiber, 1 g sugar, 10 g fat, 5.5 g saturated fat, 574 mg sodium

Breakfast Muffin Parfait

How's this for fast food: Layer protein-rich muffins, Greek yogurt, and berries in a jar, screw on the lid, and you have a healthy breakfast to go.

Makes 1 serving

2 tablespoons almond flour

1 tablespoon coconut flour

1 teaspoon ground flaxseed

½ teaspoon baking powder

Pinch of ground cardamom or cinnamon

Pinch of salt

1 egg

1 tablespoon applesauce or mashed ripe banana

1 tablespoon unsweetened almond milk

4 tablespoons fresh blueberries, divided

½ cup low-fat plain Greek yogurt

¼ teaspoon vanilla extract

1. Lightly grease a large microwaveable mug or ramekin. In a small bowl, combine the flours, flaxseed, baking powder, cardamom or cinnamon, and salt. Mix in the egg, applesauce or mashed banana, and almond milk until fully incorporated. Stir in 2 tablespoons of the blueberries. Pour the muffin mixture into the prepared mug or ramekin.

2. Microwave on high power for 1 to 1½ minutes, or until a wooden pick inserted into the center comes out clean. Set aside briefly until cool enough to handle.

3. In a small bowl, mix together the yogurt and vanilla.

4. Crumble half the muffin into the bottom of a small jar, bowl, or parfait glass. Top with half the yogurt. Repeat layers with the remaining muffin and yogurt. Top with the remaining 2 tablespoons blueberries and enjoy.

Nutrition per serving: 326 calories, 24 g protein, 21 g carbohydrates, 6 g fiber, 12 g sugar, 17 g fat, 5 g saturated fat, 533 mg sodium

Veggie-Stuffed Cheese Omelet

I always order veggie omelets when I go out for brunch—and they're typically oozing with cheese and glistening with butter. This recipe is pretty skinny thanks to just a sprinkle of flavor-packed Cheddar and a touch of oil.

Makes 1 serving

1 teaspoon olive oil or canola oil

2 tablespoons chopped red bell pepper

1 tablespoon chopped yellow or white onion

¼ cup sliced mushrooms

1 cup loosely packed baby spinach

2 eggs

1 tablespoon water

Pinch of salt

Pinch of ground black pepper

1 tablespoon shredded Cheddar cheese

1 pink grapefruit, peeled

1. In a small nonstick skillet over medium-high heat, warm the oil. Cook the bell pepper, onion, and mushrooms, stirring frequently, for 4 minutes, or until the onion is tender. Stir in the spinach and cook, stirring, for 4 minutes, or until the spinach is wilted. Transfer the vegetables to a small bowl.

2. In a separate small bowl, beat the eggs, water, salt, and black pepper with a fork or whisk until well mixed. Return the skillet to medium-high heat and pour in the egg mixture. While sliding the skillet back and forth rapidly over the heat, quickly stir the eggs with a rubber spatula to spread them continuously over the bottom of the skillet as they thicken. Let stand over the heat a few seconds to lightly brown the bottom of the omelet before removing the skillet.

3. Place the cooked vegetable mixture over half the omelet. Top with the cheese. With the spatula, fold the other half of the omelet over the vegetables. Gently slide out of the skillet onto a plate. Serve immediately with the grapefruit on the side.

Nutrition per serving: 317 calories, 17 g protein, 27 g carbohydrates, 5 g fiber, 20 g sugar, 17 g fat, 5 g saturated fat, 373 mg sodium

Protein "Muesli"

A sweet blend of oats, nuts, seeds, and raisins is a perfect match for tangy Greek yogurt. Bear Naked Fit granolas have less than 5 grams of sugar and less than 3 grams of fat per serving—which is pretty amazing for granola. Any granola that's this low in sugar and fat will do!

Makes 1 serving

1 container (5.3 ounces) low-fat plain Greek yogurt

¼ cup lower-sugar, lower-fat granola

2 tablespoons slivered almonds

1 tablespoon raisins

In a medium bowl, combine the yogurt, granola, and almonds. Top with the raisins and serve.

Nutrition per serving: 337 calories, 22 g protein, 38 g carbohydrates, 4 g fiber, 16 g sugar, 12 g fat, 3 g saturated fat, 60 mg sodium

Overnight Steel-Cut Oats and Blueberries

Here's an oatmeal recipe that's a cinch to prepare—just remember to start your oats the night before. Hemp amps up the protein.

Makes 1 serving

1 cup water

¼ cup steel-cut oats

3 tablespoons hemp seeds

Pinch of salt

⅓ cup fresh or frozen and thawed blueberries

1. In a medium saucepan over medium-high heat, bring the water to a boil. Add the oats, hemp, and salt and give it a quick stir. Cook for 1 minute.

2. Remove from the heat, stir the oats, cover, and let them sit out overnight.

3. In the morning, top with the blueberries before serving.

Nutrition per serving: 338 calories, 16 g protein, 39 g carbohydrates, 5 g fiber, 6 g sugar, 15 g fat, 1.5 g saturated fat, 155 mg sodium

Smoked Salmon and Egg Muffin

This spin on the drive-thru favorite features smoked salmon instead of sausage, light cream cheese in place of those rubbery processed cheese slices, and a healthier English muffin.

Makes 1 serving

1 sprouted grain English muffin, split and toasted

1 tablespoon reduced-fat spreadable cream cheese

1 ounce smoked salmon, sliced

1 egg

2 teaspoons milk or unsweetened almond milk

Pinch of salt

Pinch of ground black pepper

½ cup raspberries

1. Spread one half of the English muffin with the cream cheese. Top with the salmon.

2. In a small microwaveable bowl, mix the egg, milk, salt, and pepper well with a fork. Microwave on high power for 1 minute, or until set.

3. Arrange the egg on top of the salmon. Top with the other half of the muffin. Serve with the raspberries on the side.

Nutrition per serving: 388 calories, 33 g protein, 39 g carbohydrates, 10 g fiber, 4 g sugar, 11 g fat, 3.5 g saturated fat, 433 mg sodium

Easy Egg Bake

My mother makes a dish called church eggs, which is a yummy calorie bomb of a casserole made with diced white bread, a dozen eggs, shredded cheese, and sausage. This slimmed-down version is the answer to my prayers.

Makes 4 servings

10 eggs

3 tablespoons unsweetened almond milk

2 cups baby spinach

1 cup sliced red bell pepper

¼ cup chopped red onion

4 large white mushrooms, sliced

½ jalapeño pepper, seeded and finely chopped (wear plastic gloves when handling)

2 links precooked chicken sausage, chopped

Pinch of ground cumin

Pinch of red-pepper flakes

Pinch of ground black pepper

1. Preheat the oven to 350°F. Coat a 2-quart baking dish with olive oil cooking spray.

2. In a large bowl, beat together the eggs and almond milk and set aside.

3. In a large nonstick skillet over medium-high heat, cook the spinach, bell pepper, onion, mushrooms, and jalapeño for 4 minutes, or until tender. Add the sausages, cumin, red-pepper flakes, and black pepper and cook for 1 to 2 minutes, or until the sausages are heated through.

4. Add the veggie and sausage mixture to the reserved egg mixture and pour into the baking dish. Bake for 15 to 20 minutes, or until the eggs are puffed, golden, and set.

Nutrition per serving: 283 calories, 24 g protein, 11 g carbohydrates, 2 g fiber, 7 g sugar, 16 g fat, 5 g saturated fat, 448 mg sodium

Avocado Toast with Fried Eggs

Rosie in my hometown of New Canaan, Connecticut, has the most delicious avocado toast with sea salt on its menu. Top it with fried eggs for extra protein.

Makes 1 serving

½ ripe avocado, mashed

2 slices sprouted grain bread, toasted

Pinch of sea salt

2 eggs

1. Spread the avocado onto the toast and sprinkle with the salt.

2. In a medium nonstick skillet coated with olive oil cooking spray over medium-high heat, fry the eggs sunny-side up until the egg whites are just set, 3 to 4 minutes, or to your liking.

3. Place the eggs on top of the avocado toast and serve.

Nutrition per serving: 416 calories, 22 g protein, 37 g carbohydrates, 11 g fiber, 1 g sugar, 21 g fat, 4.5 g saturated fat, 396 mg sodium

Sweet and Savory Cottage Cheese Breakfast Bowl

Many of the women in this book are cottage cheese fans. Why? Because it's creamy, filling, and convenient. This recipe adds pineapple for sweetness and cashews for crunch.

Makes 1 serving

1 cup low-fat cottage cheese

3 tablespoons roasted, salted cashews

1 pineapple ring (fresh or from a can, drained), coarsely chopped

In a small bowl, stir together the cottage cheese and cashews. Top with the pineapple and serve.

Nutrition per serving: 370 calories, 31 g protein, 24 g carbohydrates, 2 g fiber, 15 g sugar, 18 g fat, 4.5 g saturated fat, 911 mg sodium

Protein Pancakes

To add protein to her breakfast, Katie Hug, a TIAO superstar who lost 137 pounds, spikes her pancakes with cottage cheese.

Makes 2 servings

½ cup liquid egg whites (or 4 egg whites)

1 egg

¼ cup old-fashioned rolled oats

¼ cup low-fat cottage cheese

½ scoop vanilla protein powder

2 teaspoons unsalted butter, divided

4 teaspoons pure maple syrup

1 cup strawberries, quartered or sliced

1. In a medium bowl, with a hand mixer, beat together the egg whites, egg, oats, cottage cheese, and protein powder.

2. In a medium nonstick skillet over medium heat, melt 1 teaspoon of the butter. Pour 3 circles of the batter (scant ¼ cup each) into the skillet and cook for 2 to 3 minutes per side, or until golden and no longer raw. Repeat with the remaining 1 teaspoon butter and the batter.

3. Serve topped with the syrup and strawberries.

Nutrition per serving: 252 calories, 21 g protein, 24 g carbohydrates, 2 g fiber, 14 g sugar, 8 g fat, 4 g saturated fat, 239 mg sodium

Mixed Greens Salad

This versatile salad complements just about any meal—from soup (opposite page and page 99) to falafel (page 97).

Makes 2 servings

---

3 cups mixed baby greens

1 tomato, halved and then cut into wedges

¼ small English cucumber, sliced

1 tablespoon balsamic vinegar or white wine vinegar

Pinch of salt

In a medium bowl, toss together the greens, tomato, and cucumber. Drizzle with the vinegar and toss again. Sprinkle with the salt and serve.

Nutrition per serving: 38 calories, 2 g protein, 7 g carbohydrates, 3 g fiber, 4 g sugar, 0 g fat, 0 g saturated fat, 99 mg sodium

Greek Lentil Soup

I love the earthiness of lentil soup. Plus, these little legumes have lots of protein, fiber, and iron. Pair the soup with a green salad for a light yet filling meal.

Makes 2 servings

1½ teaspoons olive oil

1 small onion, finely chopped

1 rib celery, chopped

1 carrot, chopped

1 clove garlic, minced

1 bay leaf

2 cups low-sodium chicken broth or vegetable broth

1 can (14.5 ounces) no-salt-added diced tomatoes

⅓ cup dried red or brown lentils, rinsed

½ teaspoon dried thyme

½ teaspoon dried basil

¼ teaspoon salt

Mixed Greens Salad (opposite page)

1. In a medium saucepan over medium heat, warm the oil. Cook the onion, celery, and carrot for 6 minutes, or until softened. Add the garlic and bay leaf and cook for 2 minutes.

2. Add the broth, tomatoes, lentils, thyme, basil, and salt. Bring to a boil. Reduce the heat to medium-low and simmer for 15 to 20 minutes, or until the lentils are tender. Remove the bay leaf before serving with the salad.

Nutrition per serving: 301 calories, 19 g protein, 44 g carbohydrates, 16 g fiber, 14 g sugar, 6 g fat, 1 g saturated fat, 604 mg sodium

Lightened-Up Chicken Salad

Many chicken salads are hidden-calorie traps, but this simple combination of protein and veggies is guaranteed to help flatten your belly.

Makes 1 serving

1½ teaspoons olive oil

4 ounces boneless, skinless chicken breast

Pinch of salt

Pinch of ground black pepper

½ recipe Mixed Greens Salad (page 92)

½ red bell pepper, cut into strips

1. In a medium skillet over medium-high heat, warm the oil. Add the chicken and sprinkle with the salt and black pepper. Cook for 8 to 10 minutes, or until golden on both sides and a thermometer inserted in the thickest portion registers 165°F. Remove to a cutting board to cool for 5 minutes and then slice. (If you'd prefer to grill the chicken, brush it with olive oil and grill over a medium flame until no longer pink.)

2. Toss the salad with the bell pepper and arrange on a plate. Top with the chicken and serve.

Nutrition per serving: 245 calories, 27 g protein, 11 g carbohydrates, 4 g fiber, 6 g sugar, 10 g fat, 1.5 g saturated fat, 378 mg sodium

Sprouted Grain Tuna Sandwich

Catch all the health benefits of tuna (protein, omega-3s, a type of B vitamin called niacin) for a fraction of the fat and calories. Choose light tuna instead of albacore (albacore contains more mercury), and whenever possible, buy sustainably caught canned tuna, which is believed to be a little healthier than regular tuna.

Makes 2 servings

1 can (about 5 ounces) wild-caught water-packed tuna, drained

1 tablespoon olive oil mayonnaise

4 slices sprouted grain bread, toasted if desired

2 leaves Boston lettuce or lettuce of choice

2 slices tomato

1. In a small bowl, mix the tuna with the mayonnaise. Spread over 2 slices of the bread or toast.

2. Top each with a lettuce leaf, a tomato slice, and the other slices of bread.

Nutrition per serving: 331 calories, 25 g protein, 31 g carbohydrates, 6 g fiber, 3 g sugar, 11 g fat, 2 g saturated fat, 453 mg sodium

Black-Eyed Pea Egg Salad

These Southern-style beans are high in protein and fiber and contain a boatload of nutrients, including magnesium, potassium, iron, and folate.

Makes 1 serving

⅔ cup canned black-eyed peas, drained and rinsed

2 hard-cooked eggs, chopped

1 tomato, chopped

¼ cup crumbled goat cheese

2 tablespoons white wine vinegar or balsamic vinegar

2 cups baby mixed greens

In a bowl, gently mix together the black-eyed peas, eggs, tomato, cheese, and vinegar. Serve immediately over the mixed greens, or refrigerate a couple hours for the flavors to meld.

Nutrition per serving: 352 calories, 24 g protein, 25 g carbohydrates, 8 g fiber, 5 g sugar, 18 g fat, 8 g saturated fat, 606 mg sodium

Falafel over Mixed Greens

This Middle Eastern staple contains fiber- and protein-packed chickpeas—and is baked (not fried) into crispy patties.

Makes 2 servings

1 can (7.5 ounces) chickpeas, rinsed and drained

½ onion, coarsely chopped

½ cup fresh parsley or cilantro

1 clove garlic

1 teaspoon fresh lemon juice

⅛ teaspoon ground cumin

Pinch of salt

Pinch of ground black pepper

¼ cup dried sprouted grain bread crumbs (see note)

¼ teaspoon baking powder

1 tablespoon tahini

1 tablespoon water

Mixed Greens Salad (page 92)

1. Preheat the broiler. Lightly grease a baking sheet with olive oil cooking spray or olive oil in a mister.

2. In a blender, pulse the chickpeas until broken up. Add the onion, parsley, garlic, lemon juice, cumin, salt, and pepper. Pulse until pasty but not pureed. Work in the bread crumbs and baking powder until the mixture firms up.

3. Form the dough into 6 golf-ball-size balls and place on the baking sheet.

4. Coat the tops of the balls lightly with olive oil cooking spray and flatten them slightly.

5. Broil for 3 minutes per side, or until the edges have a nice brown crust.

6. Mix together the tahini and water. Serve falafels over the salad with the tahini sauce drizzled over.

NOTE: To make the bread crumbs, preheat the oven to 300°F and toast 1 slice of sprouted grain bread on a baking sheet for 8 minutes per side, or until very dry. Cool completely and then run through a food processor until fine crumbs form. Store in an airtight container for up to 3 weeks.

Nutrition per serving: 214 calories, 10 g protein, 32 g carbohydrates, 8 g fiber, 6 g sugar, 7 g fat, 1 g saturated fat, 535 mg sodium

NICE RACK!

SPICE THINGS UP WITH THESE HEALTHY, POUND-SHEDDING SEASONINGS.

CHILI POWDER. This spice's secret weapon is a group of chemicals called capsaicinoids, which a review of studies, published in the journal *Appetite,*[1] found have the power to reduce appetite, boost energy expenditure by about 50 calories per day, and maximize fat burning. Use it in turkey chili, chicken tacos, and other Mexican dishes; add a dash to hot chocolate; or sprinkle it over veggies like sweet potatoes and broccoli.

GARLIC POWDER. Garlic is the spice equivalent of bacon—it makes everything taste better. (But unlike bacon, it contains almost no calories.) What's more, research[2] shows that the powder can decrease fasting blood glucose levels in people with type 2 diabetes, and it may help stoke your metabolism.

TURMERIC. Turmeric doesn't taste like much, but sprinkling a little on eggs, rice, or veggies can shrink your waistline, found a study in the journal *Food & Function.*[3] The burnt orange spice, which is a staple in Indian cuisine, contains a molecule that helps burn sugar instead of storing it as fat.

GROUND CINNAMON. As long as you're not eating it baked into snickerdoodles or apple pie, this earthy spice can help you shed pounds. In a study in the *Journal of the Academy of Nutrition and Dietetics,*[4] researchers served one group of study participants cereal spiked with 6 grams of cinnamon and another group cereal sans the spice—and then measured their blood glucose levels 15, 30, 60, and 120 minutes after eating. They found the cinnamon group had lower blood glucose levels than the regular-cereal eaters at every time increment—and less sugar floating around in your system means less sugar around to be stored as fat.

GROUND GINGER. Ginger has a lot going for it: It's been shown to alleviate nausea and pain, enhance digestion, reduce cholesterol, and improve lipid (fat) metabolism, and it may even help prevent colon cancer. Add this pleasantly pungent spice to smoothies, tea, and stir-fries, or use it as a rub for meats.

Pumpkin and White Bean Soup

Fiber- and vitamin A–filled pumpkin tastes as delicious in this soup as it does in bread, pie, and lattes. Skip the yogurt if you want to make it vegan and opt for pea or hemp protein powder.

Makes 4 servings

1 can (15 ounces) pumpkin

2 cups low-sodium vegetable broth

1 can (13.5 ounces) unsweetened coconut milk

1 can (15 ounces) cannellini beans, drained and rinsed

¼ cup protein powder

1 teaspoon crushed dried sage

¼ teaspoon salt, plus more to taste

¼ teaspoon ground black pepper, plus more to taste

¼ cup low-fat plain Greek yogurt

4 teaspoons toasted pumpkin seeds

4 lime wedges (optional)

1. In a medium saucepan over medium heat, combine the pumpkin, broth, and coconut milk. Stir in the beans, protein powder, sage, salt, and pepper. Bring to a simmer and cook, stirring occasionally, for 5 to 8 minutes, or until heated through.

2. Taste and adjust the seasonings if necessary. Divide the soup among 4 bowls, dollop with the yogurt, sprinkle with the pumpkin seeds, and serve with the lime wedges, if desired.

Nutrition per serving: 333 calories, 15 g protein, 26 g carbohydrates, 8 g fiber, 7 g sugar, 20 g fat, 15.5 g saturated fat, 440 mg sodium

Crab and Avocado Salad

This citrusy salad is light, refreshing, and full of low-fat, low-calorie crab, which is high in protein, vitamins (like A and C), and minerals (like copper and zinc).

Makes 4 servings

- 1 can (16 ounces) crab claw meat, drained
- 1 can (20 ounces) pineapple tidbits in juice, drained
- ½ cup thinly sliced celery
- ⅓ cup diced red bell pepper
- ⅓ cup sliced water chestnuts, drained
- ¼ cup slivered almonds
- 2 teaspoons fresh lemon juice
- 1 teaspoon curry powder
- 4 cups mixed greens
- 1 avocado, sliced

1. In a medium bowl, gently combine the crabmeat, pineapple, celery, pepper, water chestnuts, and almonds. Add the lemon juice and curry powder and mix well.

2. Divide the greens among 4 plates. Top with ¼ of the crab salad and ¼ of the avocado.

Nutrition per serving: 258 calories, 23 g protein, 22 g carbohydrates, 6 g fiber, 15 g sugar, 10 g fat, 1 g saturated fat, 450 mg sodium

Chicken Paillard

Dress up grilled chicken with a peppery arugula salad doused in a light lemon vinaigrette.

Makes 1 serving

1 thinly sliced boneless, skinless chicken breast (4 ounces), see note

Pinch of salt

Pinch of ground black pepper

1 tablespoon olive oil

Juice of ½ lemon (2 tablespoons)

1 cup baby arugula

5 grape or cherry tomatoes, halved

Freshly shaved Parmesan cheese

1. Coat the grates of a grill with olive oil cooking spray. Preheat the grill to medium heat.

2. Sprinkle the chicken with the salt and pepper. Grill for 8 minutes total, turning once, or until cooked through and nice grill marks appear. Remove to a plate.

3. In a small bowl, whisk together the oil and lemon juice.

4. Place the arugula and tomatoes over the chicken breast and drizzle with the vinaigrette. Top with a few shavings of Parmesan.

NOTE: If you have trouble finding thinly sliced chicken breasts (called cutlets), take a regular chicken breast and place it between 2 pieces of plastic wrap or in a resealable plastic bag. Pound with a meat mallet or heavy skillet until it's an even ½" thick.

Nutrition per serving: 302 calories, 28 g protein, 6 g carbohydrates, 1 g fiber, 3 g sugar, 19 g fat, 3.5 g saturated fat, 400 mg sodium

Chicken Salad with Grapes, Almonds, and Carrots

A skinnier spin on the classic Waldorf salad.

Makes 4 servings

1 pound boneless, skinless chicken breasts

⅓ cup slivered almonds

⅔ cup low-fat plain Greek yogurt

2 tablespoons olive oil mayonnaise

1 tablespoon fresh lemon juice

1 cup sliced celery

1 cup green or red grapes, halved

1 carrot, grated

2 cups baby arugula

1. Bring a large saucepan of lightly salted water to a boil over high heat. Reduce the heat to a rolling simmer and cook the chicken for 20 minutes, or until a thermometer inserted in the thickest portion registers 165°F. Remove from the water and let cool for 10 minutes before cutting into ¾" cubes.

2. Meanwhile, preheat the oven to 350°F. Place the almonds on a baking sheet and bake 8 to 10 minutes, or until golden and fragrant. Remove from the oven and cool completely.

3. In a large bowl, mix together the yogurt, mayonnaise, and lemon juice. Add the chicken, almonds, celery, grapes, and carrot and thoroughly combine. Cover and let sit for 1 hour for the flavors to blend. (Refrigerate if holding for any longer.)

4. Divide the arugula among 4 plates and top each with an equal portion of the chicken salad.

Nutrition per serving: 370 calories, 31 g protein, 14 g carbohydrates, 3 g fiber, 9 g sugar, 22 g fat, 5 g saturated fat, 159 mg sodium

Easy Salmon Patties

Oats and olive oil cooking spray let you have your (salmon) cake and eat it, too.

Makes 4 servings

1 can (14–15 ounces) boneless, skinless pink salmon, drained

¼ cup cornmeal

¼ cup old-fashioned rolled oats, ground until fine in a food processor or coffee grinder

¼ cup finely chopped yellow onion

1 egg

3 tablespoons olive oil mayonnaise

2 recipes Mixed Greens Salad (page 92)

1. In a medium bowl, flake the salmon. Mix in the cornmeal, oats, onion, egg, and mayonnaise. Form into 4 equal-size patties, about ½″ thick.

2. In a large nonstick skillet coated with olive oil cooking spray over medium-high heat, cook the patties for 6 to 8 minutes, turning once, or until golden brown on both sides.

3. Divide the salad among 4 plates and top each with 1 patty.

Nutrition per serving: 314 calories, 27 g protein, 22 g carbohydrates, 5 g fiber, 5 g sugar, 13 g fat, 2 g saturated fat, 494 mg sodium

"We Did It!"

THEIR STORY: Identical twins Jen Kelley and Kelly McCarthy did everything together, including gain weight. They ate out constantly and regularly indulged in heavy foods like chicken Alfredo—with a side of fries.

WAKE-UP CALL: Spotting an unflattering Facebook picture of herself spurred Jen to take action in 2009. "I realized how awful it was to be this young and unhealthy," she says. Jen decided to hit the gym and urged Kelly to join her.

SUCCESS SECRETS: With the help of a trainer, Jen and Kelly began a workout program consisting of running, biking, and strength training, which they tackled four times a week for an hour. They hit the kitchen and broke out the slow cooker, using it to create lighter versions of old favorites, like Mexican chicken and rice. They packed protein into their diets with egg-white omelets and bananas with peanut butter. By January 2013, both had lost 70 pounds. When Kelly developed a running injury, they took up swimming instead and lifted heavier weights during strength sessions—and shed 20 more pounds apiece. Now they're all about boot-camp class: "Throwing down ropes and hoisting barbells over your head is just awesome," says Kelly.

Both sisters say that having a workout buddy, whether it's your sibling, partner, or coworker is key to maintaining success. "I definitely attribute my support system for my weight loss," Jen says. "My sister and husband are there for me on good days and bad. If I need motivation to workout or a workout buddy, they're there!" The twins even shared healthy recipes to stay on track. "I learned how to make my favorite foods the healthy way!" Kelly says. "Making my food not only saved money, but calories."

Their advice to fitness newbies? "Start small. Sometimes the biggest mistake you can make is going too hard, too fast," Jen says.

NAMES: **Jen Kelley and Kelly McCarthy**

AGES: **31**

HOMETOWNS: **Warren, Rhode Island, and Norton, Massachusetts, respectively**

BEFORE WEIGHTS: **254**

AFTER WEIGHTS: **164**

DINNER

Spaghetti Squash with Turkey Tomato Sauce

Spaghetti squash, which is high in potassium and vitamin A and low in calories and carbs, looks and tastes enough like pasta to sub for noodles with this turkey meat sauce. Look for a tomato sauce that doesn't contain added sugar.

Makes 1 serving

½ small spaghetti squash (about 3 pounds), halved lengthwise

¼ cup water

5 ounces lean (7% fat) ground turkey

½ cup chopped yellow or white onion

1 clove garlic, minced

1 teaspoon dried basil

⅛ teaspoon salt

⅛ teaspoon ground black pepper

½ cup tomato sauce or puree

1. Put the squash pieces, cut-side down, in a microwaveable dish and add the water. Microwave on high power for 10 minutes, or until a fork easily pierces the skin.

2. Meanwhile, in a medium nonstick skillet over medium heat, cook the turkey and onion for 5 minutes, or until the turkey is no longer pink and the onion begins to soften. Add the garlic, basil, salt, and pepper and cook for 1 minute.

3. Stir in the tomato sauce, reduce the heat to low, and simmer for 5 minutes, or until the sauce is heated through and slightly thickened and the onion is soft.

4. Scrape out the "spaghetti" (squash) seeds and strands with a fork into a large bowl. Dish out 2 cups for this meal (save the rest) and top with the turkey tomato sauce.

Nutrition per serving: 360 calories, 33 g protein, 41 g carbohydrates, 8 g fiber, 19 g sugar, 10 g fat, 3 g saturated fat, 511 mg sodium

Pork Tenderloin with Butternut Squash and Steamed Spinach

Lean and healthy, the "other white meat" is a tasty alternative to chicken, especially when paired with nutrient-dense sides like squash and spinach.

Makes 4 servings

½ butternut squash (about 1½ pounds), peeled, seeded, and cut into wedges

Salt, to taste

Ground black pepper, to taste

1 pound pork tenderloin, trimmed

1 bag (5 or 6 ounces) baby spinach, rinsed in a colander

1 teaspoon white wine vinegar

1. Preheat the oven to 425°F.

2. Place the squash on a baking sheet. Lightly coat with olive oil in a spray mister and sprinkle with salt and pepper.

3. Bake for 10 minutes. Remove from the oven, toss the squash, and move to one side of the baking sheet.

4. Coat the pork with olive oil spray and sprinkle with salt and pepper. Carefully set on the other half of the baking sheet. Return to the oven and bake for 10 to 12 minutes, or until the squash is tender and golden and the pork is cooked through. (A thermometer inserted in the center of the pork reaches 145°F.)

5. Remove from the oven and cover with foil to keep warm as you prepare the spinach.

6. In a large nonstick skillet over medium heat, add the wet spinach, a few handfuls at a time, covering between additions. Steam for 2 minutes, or until all the spinach is wilted. Sprinkle with the vinegar, salt, and pepper.

7. Slice the pork. Divide equally among 4 plates and serve with equal portions of the squash and spinach.

Nutrition per serving: 213 calories, 26 g protein, 21 g carbohydrates, 5 g fiber, 3 g sugar, 4 g fat, 1 g saturated fat, 267 mg sodium

Beef and Kale Stir-Fry

One of our weight loss superstars, Katie Russell, who dropped 93 pounds, started making kale stir-fries instead of ordering Chinese takeout. The secret to an easy stir-fry is having all of your ingredients chopped and ready to go before you turn on the heat. For a heartier meal, serve it over $\frac{1}{2}$ cup cooked brown rice.

Makes 4 servings

½ cup low-sodium beef broth or vegetable broth

⅓ cup reduced-sodium tamari or reduced-sodium soy sauce

3 tablespoons rice vinegar

½ teaspoon red-pepper flakes

1 pound flank steak, cut into thin strips across the grain

2 tablespoons tapioca starch or cornstarch

2 tablespoons peanut, canola, or grape-seed oil, divided

8 ounces button mushrooms, quartered

2 cloves garlic, minced

4 cups chopped kale or baby kale

1 can (8 ounces) water chestnuts, drained

1 teaspoon sesame oil (optional)

2 scallions, thinly sliced

1. In a resealable plastic bag, combine the broth, tamari or soy sauce, vinegar, red-pepper flakes, and beef. (Alternatively, in a large bowl, whisk the liquids and red-pepper flakes, add the beef, and cover.) Refrigerate for at least 15 minutes.

2. In a small bowl, combine 2 tablespoons of the marinade with the tapioca starch or cornstarch until no lumps remain. Set aside.

3. In a large skillet or wok over medium-high heat, warm 1 tablespoon of the peanut, canola, or grape-seed oil. Using a slotted spoon, remove the steak from the marinade, reserving the marinade, and add the steak to the skillet or wok. Cook, stirring frequently, for 2 to 3 minutes, or until browned. Remove with a slotted spoon and set aside.

4. Add the remaining 1 tablespoon oil to the skillet. Add the mushrooms and cook for 3 to 4 minutes, or until they release their juices. Add the garlic and cook for 1 minute, or until fragrant. Add the kale, water chestnuts, and reserved marinade from the bag and stir to combine. Cook, stirring, for 3 minutes, or until the kale is wilted and the mushrooms have cooked. Add the reserved starch-marinade mixture and cook for 2 minutes, or until the sauce has thickened. Add in the reserved steak and sesame oil (if desired) and toss to combine.

5. Divide among 4 bowls and sprinkle on the scallions to serve.

Nutrition per serving: 352 calories, 32 g protein, 18 g carbohydrates, 3 g fiber, 3 g sugar, 17 g fat, 5 g saturated fat, 1,037 mg sodium

Maple Pork with Apples

This fall-harvest dish is sweetened with maple syrup, which contains plant-derived compounds called polyphenols that can help slow aging, and the immunity-boosting minerals zinc and manganese.

Makes 4 servings

2 tablespoons unsalted butter

4 bone-in pork loin chops, ½" thick (about 2 pounds total)

Pinch of salt

Pinch of ground black pepper

12 young carrots (with tops), halved lengthwise

1 apple, cut into 8 wedges

¼ cup maple syrup

1. In a large skillet over medium heat, melt the butter. Sprinkle the chops with the salt and pepper. Add the chops and brown for 2 minutes, turn, and brown for 2 minutes more.

2. Reduce the heat to medium-low and add the carrots, apple, and syrup. Cover and cook until the carrots and apple are tender and the pork is desired doneness, about 8 minutes for medium or until the carrots and apple are tender and a thermometer inserted in the center of a chop registers 145°F. Transfer the chops, carrots, and apple to a platter.

3. Bring the syrup mixture to a gentle boil and cook, uncovered, for 1 to 2 minutes, or until thickened.

4. Pour the mixture over the chops and serve.

Nutrition per serving: 366 calories, 36 g protein, 29 g carbohydrates, 4 g fiber, 23 g sugar, 12 g fat, 5.5 g saturated fat, 200 mg sodium

Salmon with Sautéed Tomatoes and Quinoa

Salmon is full of omega-3s, vitamin D, selenium, and protein, and quinoa contains protein, fiber, iron, copper, and other vitamins and minerals. Tomatoes aren't too shabby either—they pack lycopene, a plant pigment that can help prevent cancer and other diseases. (Cooking tomatoes boosts the health benefits.)

Makes 4 servings

1 cup dried quinoa, rinsed

4 teaspoons olive oil, divided

2 pints grape or cherry tomatoes

½ teaspoon salt, divided

¼ cup chopped fresh dill

4 skinless salmon fillets (4–6 ounces each)

¼ teaspoon ground black pepper

1. Cook the quinoa according to package directions.

2. Meanwhile, in a large nonstick skillet over medium-high heat, warm 2 teaspoons of the oil. Cook the tomatoes with ¼ teaspoon of the salt for 4 to 6 minutes, or until soft. Stir in the dill and transfer to a serving plate.

3. Season the salmon with the pepper and the remaining ¼ teaspoon salt. Wipe out the skillet and warm the remaining 2 teaspoons oil over medium heat. Cook the salmon for 4 minutes per side, or until opaque.

4. Serve each fillet with 1 cup of the tomatoes and ¾ cup of the cooked quinoa.

Nutrition per serving: 459 calories, 31 g protein, 33 g carbohydrates, 5 g fiber, 6 g sugar, 23 g fat, 4.5 g saturated fat, 368 mg sodium

Zesty Chicken with Asparagus and Sweet Potato

This chicken recipe features sweet potato (which is high in vitamins, especially vitamin A, and carotenoids, plant compounds that act as antioxidants and are associated with immunity and heart disease prevention) and asparagus (which is full of vitamins K, C, and E, plus folate, beta-carotene, zinc, and manganese).

Makes 2 servings

2 boneless, skinless chicken breasts (4 ounces each)

4 teaspoons olive oil, divided

Juice of ½ lemon

1 clove garlic, minced

1 teaspoon lemon-pepper seasoning

½ teaspoon salt, divided

½ teaspoon dried oregano

1 sweet potato

½ bunch asparagus, woody ends snapped off and stalks cut into bite-size pieces

½ cup water

½ lemon, cut into wedges, for garnish

2 teaspoons salted butter

1. Place the chicken breasts in a resealable plastic bag or between 2 pieces of plastic wrap. Pound with a meat mallet or heavy skillet until they are an even ½" thick.

2. To the bag, add 1 tablespoon of the oil, the lemon juice, garlic, lemon-pepper seasoning, ¼ teaspoon of the salt, and the oregano. Seal the bag and turn a few times to mix and evenly coat the chicken. (Alternatively, mix in a bowl and add the chicken, turning to coat.)

3. Marinate the chicken in the refrigerator for 2 hours, turning the bag often (or using a fork or tongs to turn the chicken if in a bowl).

4. Prick the potato all over with a fork. Microwave on high power for 8 to 10 minutes, or until tender.

5. Meanwhile, remove the chicken from the marinade, discarding the marinade. In a large nonstick skillet over medium heat, cook the chicken for 3 to 4 minutes on each side, or until cooked through.

6. While the chicken cooks, in a separate skillet over medium-high heat, combine the asparagus and water and bring to a boil. Cook the asparagus for 5 minutes, or until bright green and tender. Drain the water, drizzle with the remaining oil, and sprinkle with the remaining ¼ teaspoon salt.

7. Serve each piece of chicken with the lemon wedges, half the asparagus, and half the sweet potato with 1 teaspoon of the butter.

Nutrition per serving: 310 calories, 27 g protein, 15 g carbohydrates, 3 g fiber, 5 g sugar, 16 g fat, 4.5 g saturated fat, 844 mg sodium

Bison Burgers

Leaner than beef, bison makes for a better burger—especially when perched on a sprouted grain bun.

Makes 4 servings

1 egg

1 pound ground bison

½ cup old-fashioned rolled oats

½ cup chopped baby spinach

⅓ cup chopped yellow onion

2 tablespoons Mexican blend cheese

Pinch of ground black pepper

4 cups broccoli florets

½ cup water

Pinch of salt

Toppings such as lettuce, tomato, onion, salsa (optional)

2 sprouted grain burger buns, halved

1. In a large bowl, whisk the egg. Add the bison, oats, spinach, onion, cheese, and pepper. Mix with your hands until well blended. Form into 4 patties, about ½″ thick.

2. Preheat a grill or nonstick skillet over medium-high heat. Cook the burgers until desired level of doneness, turning once. For a medium-rare burger, grill about 3 minutes per side.

3. In a medium saucepan or skillet over medium-high heat, combine the broccoli and water. Cover and bring to a boil. Steam for 3 minutes, or until bright green and slightly tender. Drain and sprinkle with the salt.

4. Serve the burgers with condiments of your choice, if desired, each over ½ of a bun, with the steamed broccoli on the side.

Nutrition per serving: 436 calories, 32 g protein, 29 g carbohydrates, 7 g fiber, 1 g sugar, 22 g fat, 9 g saturated fat, 263 mg sodium

Fish Tacos with Mango Salsa

Fish tacos are my seafood restaurant go-to meal. These aren't battered, fried, and drizzled with chipotle mayo (sigh), but they still taste pretty delicious thanks to a bright, fruity salsa.

Makes 4 servings

3 tablespoons fresh lime juice, divided

2 teaspoons olive oil

½ teaspoon chili powder

1 jalapeño pepper, finely chopped (wear plastic gloves when handling), divided

1 pound cod, tilapia, or other flaky white fish

2 plum tomatoes, chopped

1 mango, chopped

1 avocado, chopped

¼ red or white onion, chopped

Pinch of salt

8 corn taco shells or tortillas

1. In a large bowl, whisk together 1 tablespoon of the lime juice, the oil, chili powder, and half of the jalapeño. Add the fish, turn to coat, and marinate for 30 minutes.

2. In a separate bowl, combine the tomatoes, mango, avocado, onion, salt, the remaining 2 tablespoons lime juice, and the remaining jalapeño. Set aside for the flavors to meld.

3. Remove the fish from the marinade, discarding the marinade. In a large nonstick skillet over medium-high heat, cook the fish for 3 to 4 minutes per side, or until opaque.

4. Separate the fish into 4 portions and divide each portion between 2 taco shells or tortillas. Top each with a heaping spoonful of the salsa.

Nutrition per serving: 362 calories, 24 g protein, 36 g carbohydrates, 6 g fiber, 13 g sugar, 15 g fat, 2 g saturated fat, 203 mg sodium

Gluten-Free Turkey Meat Loaf Minis

Lean ground turkey and quinoa flakes trim the fat (and calories) from this classic comfort food. Look for a brand of barbecue sauce that's low in sugar (less than 7 grams per serving).

Makes 3 servings

1 egg

1 pound lean (7% fat) ground turkey

½ apple, peeled and finely chopped

⅓ cup quinoa flakes, quick oats, or cornmeal

3 tablespoons barbecue sauce

A few shakes of Montreal steak spice

1 recipe Mixed Greens Salad (page 92)

1. Preheat the oven to 375°F. Coat half of a 12-cup muffin pan with olive oil cooking spray.

2. In a large bowl, beat the egg. Add the turkey, apple, quinoa flakes or quick oats or cornmeal, barbecue sauce, and spice mix and use your fingers to gently combine.

3. Press the mixture into the 6 prepared muffin cups. Bake for 30 minutes, or until a thermometer reads 165°F. Allow to cool for 10 minutes before serving 2 "minis" with 1 heaping cup of the green salad per person.

Nutrition per serving: 322 calories, 34 g protein, 21 g carbohydrates, 3 g fiber, 9 g sugar, 12 g fat, 3 g saturated fat, 332 mg sodium

Skirt Steak with Mashed Cauliflower

Think of this as a slim version of meat and potatoes, featuring lean beef and creamy mashed cauliflower in place of spuds.

Makes 4 servings

¼ cup + 1½ teaspoons olive oil

¼ cup balsamic vinegar

2 tablespoons fresh rosemary

2 cloves garlic, minced

½ teaspoon salt, plus more to taste

½ teaspoon ground black pepper, plus more to taste

1 pound skirt steak, trimmed

½ head cauliflower, trimmed and cut into small florets (3–4 cups)

1. In a large resealable plastic bag, combine the ¼ cup oil, vinegar, rosemary, garlic, salt, and pepper. Add the steak, seal, and turn over a few times to coat. Refrigerate, turning the bag occasionally, for 3 to 4 hours.

2. When ready to eat, bring a pot of lightly salted water to a boil. Preheat a grill to medium-high heat.

3. Add the cauliflower to the boiling water and cook for 10 minutes, or until very tender. Drain, reserving ¼ cup of the cooking liquid. In a food processor, add the cooked cauliflower and the 1½ teaspoons oil. Puree until smooth, adding the reserved water, 1 tablespoon at a time, if needed. (Alternatively, transfer to a bowl and mash with a potato masher.) Season with salt and pepper to taste.

4. Remove the steak from the bag, shake off the excess marinade, and grill until desired doneness, 4 to 5 minutes per side for medium-rare steak.

5. Remove the steak from the grill and slice it thinly against the grain. Serve with the mashed cauliflower.

Nutrition per serving: 260 calories, 25 g protein, 5 g carbohydrates, 2 g fiber, 2 g sugar, 15 g fat, 4.5 g saturated fat, 223 mg sodium

Seafood Rice

If you like paella, you'll love this dish, which combines mild, protein-rich cod and shrimp with healthy seasonings and fiber-filled brown rice. Don't let the number of ingredients intimidate you—it's mostly seasonings you already have sitting in your spice rack.

Makes 6 servings

1 tablespoon olive oil

1 yellow onion, chopped

1 clove garlic, chopped

2 teaspoons curry powder

1 teaspoon ground cumin

1 teaspoon salt

½ teaspoon chili powder

¼ teaspoon ground black pepper

¼ teaspoon ground cinnamon

¼ teaspoon ground cloves

1¼ cups brown rice

2½ cups boiling water

1 pound cod, cut into 1" pieces

½ pound large shrimp, peeled and deveined

1 cup frozen peas, thawed

1 cup frozen corn kernels, thawed

1 tablespoon fresh lime juice

1. In a 4-quart saucepan over medium heat, warm the oil. Cook the onion, garlic, curry powder, cumin, salt, chili powder, pepper, cinnamon, and cloves, stirring continuously, for 1 minute.

2. Stir in the rice, mixing until well coated with the spices and oil. Pour in the boiling water, cover, reduce the heat to low, and simmer for 25 minutes.

3. Add the fish, shrimp, peas, and corn. Stir thoroughly. Cover and cook for 8 to 10 minutes, or until the fish is opaque and the rice is tender.

4. Fluff the rice with a fork and sprinkle with the lime juice before serving.

Nutrition per serving: 300 calories, 23 g protein, 41 g carbohydrates, 4 g fiber, 3 g sugar, 5 g fat, 0.5 g saturated fat, 648 mg sodium

Citrus-Ginger Pork Roast with Fruit

Plan ahead for this tangy Asian take on pork roast. You'll need to marinate the meat overnight and then let it sit on the grill for an hour. But it will yield plenty of leftovers, saving you time the next day.

Makes 8 servings

1¼ cups orange juice (fresh preferred)

Juice of 1 lemon

Juice of 1 lime

1 tablespoon soy sauce or tamari

1 tablespoon grated fresh ginger

1 teaspoon Dijon mustard

1 clove garlic, minced

1 teaspoon ground black pepper

1 center-cut, boneless pork loin roast (about 3 pounds)

3 star fruit, sliced, or ½ small papaya, peeled and diced

1 cup diced fresh (or canned and drained) pineapple

2 kiwifruit, peeled and sliced into wedges

1. In a large resealable plastic bag, combine the orange juice, lemon juice, lime juice, soy sauce or tamari, ginger, mustard, garlic, and pepper. Add the pork, seal the bag, and refrigerate for 12 to 24 hours, turning the bag several times.

2. Place a drip pan beneath the grates on one side of the grill. Preheat the other side to medium-low heat. (The nonheat side should be over the drip pan.)

3. Drain the marinade from the roast into a saucepan and bring to a boil. Boil for 5 minutes and then set aside.

4. Place the roast on the cool side of the grill, over the drip pan. Close the grill and cook, basting occasionally with the reserved marinade, for 1 hour, or until a thermometer inserted in the center registers 145°F. Remove from the grill and tent with foil for 10 minutes before carving.

5. In a medium bowl, combine the star fruit or papaya, pineapple, and kiwi. Serve alongside the pork.

Nutrition per serving: 271 calories, 39 g protein, 13 g carbohydrates, 2 g fiber, 9 g sugar, 7 g fat, 2 g saturated fat, 261 mg sodium

Turkey Lettuce Wraps

I saw food writer Mark Bittman whipping up these wraps on the *TODAY* show one morning and decided to make my own version, which uses coleslaw mix to cut down on chopping.

Makes 4 servings

2 tablespoons peanut, canola, or grape-seed oil, divided

1 tablespoon grated fresh ginger

3 cloves garlic, minced

1 scallion, chopped

1 bag (14–16 ounces) coleslaw mix with carrots

1 cup button mushrooms, sliced

½ pound ground turkey

½ cup low-sodium chicken broth or vegetable broth

2 tablespoons soy sauce or tamari

Juice of 1 lime

2 tablespoons cashews, chopped

8–12 large leaves lettuce

1. In a large nonstick skillet or wok over medium-high heat, warm 1 tablespoon of the oil. Cook the ginger, garlic, and scallion for 30 seconds, or until fragrant.

2. Add the coleslaw mix and mushrooms, increase the heat to high, and cook, stirring continuously, for 6 to 8 minutes, or until the mushrooms release some of their liquid and the coleslaw is soft. Remove to a plate.

3. Reduce the heat to medium-high and warm the remaining 1 tablespoon oil. Cook the turkey, stirring occasionally, for 5 minutes, or until no longer pink.

4. Add the cooked vegetables, broth, soy sauce or tamari, and lime juice. Cook, scraping up any bits from the bottom of the pan, for 2 to 3 minutes, or until the liquid is reduced. Stir in the cashews.

5. Scoop the turkey mixture into the lettuce leaves and serve 2 or 3 leaves per person (depending on the size of the leaves).

Nutrition per serving: 222 calories, 15 g protein, 11 g carbohydrates, 3 g fiber, 5 g sugar, 13 g fat, 2.5 g saturated fat, 727 mg sodium

Honey-Brined Pork Chops

These flavorful, lean chops are glazed in honey (known to be antibacterial and antioxidant rich), piney rosemary, and grated lemon peel. Make sure to allow 4 to 6 hours for the chops to brine.

Makes 4 servings

3 cups cold water

¼ cup kosher salt

¼ cup honey

4 boneless pork chops
(6 ounces each),
pounded to ¾" thickness

2 cloves garlic, chopped

Grated peel of 1 lemon

1 tablespoon finely
chopped fresh rosemary

⅛ teaspoon ground black
pepper

2 teaspoons canola oil

2 recipes Mixed Greens
Salad (page 92)

1. In a medium saucepan, bring the water, salt, and honey to a boil, stirring until the salt and honey dissolve. Remove from the heat and cool completely. Pour over the pork chops in a shallow dish, cover, and refrigerate for 4 to 6 hours.

2. Preheat the oven to 400°F. Remove the pork from the brine and pat dry with paper towels. In a small bowl, mix the garlic, lemon peel, rosemary, and pepper. Season both sides of the pork with the mixture.

3. In a large ovenproof skillet over medium-high heat, warm the oil. Sear the pork for 2 minutes, flipping halfway through. Transfer the skillet to the oven and roast the pork for 8 to 10 minutes, or until a thermometer in the center of the chop registers 145°F. Allow to rest for 3 minutes before serving with the salad.

Nutrition per serving: 329 calories, 39 g protein, 9 g carbohydrates, 3 g fiber, 5 g sugar, 15 g fat, 4.5 g saturated fat, 481 mg sodium

OIL SMACKDOWN

THESE COOKING COMPANIONS ALL HAVE THEIR OWN HEALTH BENEFITS. WHICH ONE IS BEST DEPENDS ON WHAT YOU PLAN TO USE IT FOR. BECAUSE MOST RING IN AT AROUND 120 CALORIES PER TABLESPOON, USE THEM SPARINGLY.

OLIVE OIL. Olive oil is made by pressing the juice out of ripe olives, and it contains monounsaturated fats, which can help lower your risk of heart disease. Extra-virgin olive oil is the oil that comes from the first pressing of olives. It is the most pure and flavorful type of olive oil and contains the most antioxidants. Drizzle it over veggies and salad, or toss it with pasta.

PEANUT OIL. High in heart-healthy monounsaturated fat and vitamin E, this oil has a high smoke point, meaning you can cook it at high heat before it begins to break down, or burn. It adds a nutty flavor to Asian dishes, and it's great for frying—but since you won't be doing any frying here, forget I mentioned it.

COCONUT OIL. Coconut oil contains saturated fat, which can contribute to heart disease, but it packs a type of saturated fat called lauric acid that the body may burn fast for energy. That may explain why when Brazilian researchers[5] put a group of study subjects on a low-calorie diet and had them walk for 50 minutes each day, and gave one group a daily coconut oil supplement and the other group a daily soybean oil supplement, only the coconut oil eaters ended up with a smaller waistline after 12 weeks. This trendy oil has a vaguely sweet flavor that won't mix well with certain foods; use it for baking, in soups and smoothies, or for sautéing veggies or fish.

CANOLA OIL. Like Switzerland, canola is known for its neutrality. It has a bland flavor that disappears into whatever you are cooking; it has a high smoke point; and it can be used to bake, sauté, or fry. Pressed from the rapeseed plant, it packs polyunsaturated and monounsaturated fats, which can help reduce your risk of heart disease, and it is high in a type of omega-3 fatty acid called alpha-linolenic acid (ALA), which our bodies can't make.

GRAPE SEED OIL. Think of this oil as a best supporting actor—it helps the star (your food) shine without overshadowing it. Its high smoke point makes it great for sautéing, roasting, and frying, yet it's light and delicate enough to be drizzled over salad. Plus, it is high in "good" polyunsaturated fat, is an excellent source of vitamin E, and may help lower cholesterol.

SESAME OIL. Subtly nutty in flavor, this oil is popular in Asian dishes like stir-fries. It has a high smoke point, and research shows that it may help lower blood pressure.[6]

COOKING SPRAY. Coating your food with something resembling a can of hairspray doesn't exactly feel healthy, but cooking spray (which is nearly calorie-free) can come in handy when you need a nonstick surface for scrambling eggs or crisping up a grilled cheese—or need to "grease" a cake pan and would rather not use butter. Choose one that contains actual oil (and doesn't have creepy ingredients like diacetyl or propellants like butane and isobutene). Or better yet, buy a mister at your hardware store and fill it with your favorite oil. It may cost you a few more calories than the sprays, but not enough to make a difference.

Mock Chicken Fried Rice

Even my picky, junk food–loving children are fooled by this clever play on fried rice, which is inspired by a Weight Watchers recipe. My fried rice has broccoli, plus eggs and a dash of oil to add a little more fat and flavor.

Makes 6 servings

3 teaspoons canola oil, divided

2 eggs

½ cup chopped scallions

2 cloves garlic, minced

12 ounces boneless, skinless chicken breast, cut into ½" cubes

½ cup chopped carrots

½ cup chopped broccoli

2 cups cooked brown rice, warmed

½ cup frozen peas, thawed

¼ cup soy sauce or tamari

1. In a nonstick skillet over medium-high heat, warm 1 teaspoon of the oil. Cook the eggs, stirring continuously, for 2 to 3 minutes, or until scrambled and cooked to your liking. Remove the eggs to a plate.

2. Warm the remaining oil. Cook the scallions and garlic for 2 minutes. Add the chicken, carrots, and broccoli and cook for 5 to 8 minutes, or until the chicken is cooked through and the veggies are tender.

3. Stir in the reserved eggs, rice, peas, and soy sauce or tamari. Cook until heated through, stirring occasionally. Serve.

Nutrition per serving: 208 calories, 18 g protein, 20 g carbohydrates, 2 g fiber, 2 g sugar, 6 g fat, 1 g saturated fat, 889 mg sodium

Chicken Shirataki Noodle Stir-Fry

This recipe is a riff on that takeout classic lo mein, and it is equally delicious with shrimp—just cut the cooking time in Step 3 to 3 minutes.

Makes 2 servings

1 tablespoon soy sauce or tamari

1 tablespoon water

1 teaspoon honey

1 teaspoon sesame oil

½–1 teaspoon sriracha hot sauce

2 teaspoons canola oil

1 clove garlic, minced

1 teaspoon grated fresh ginger

½ pound chicken breast cutlets, cut into 1" pieces

1 package (16 ounces) frozen stir-fry vegetables

1 package (8 ounces) shirataki fettuccine noodles, drained and rinsed

1. In a small bowl, combine the soy sauce or tamari, water, honey, sesame oil, and hot sauce. Set aside.

2. In a large nonstick skillet over medium-high heat, warm the canola oil. Cook the garlic and ginger for 30 seconds, or until fragrant.

3. Add the chicken and cook for 6 minutes, or until cooked through. Remove the chicken to a plate.

4. Add the frozen vegetables to the skillet and cook for 4 minutes, or until brightly colored and heated through.

5. Add the cooked chicken, the noodles, and the reserved sauce. Reduce the heat to medium-low and cook, stirring, for 2 minutes, or until the noodles are heated through. Serve.

Nutrition per serving: 321 calories, 29 g protein, 22 g carbohydrates, 6 g fiber, 9 g sugar, 11 g fat, 1.5 g saturated fat, 800 mg sodium

SNACKS

Hummus and Veggies

Hummus is made from chickpeas, which are an important source of protein and fiber. And it's super easy to make at home!

Makes 6 servings (¼ cup each)

1 can (15 ounces) chickpeas, drained and rinsed

¼ cup tahini

2 tablespoons low-fat plain Greek yogurt

1 clove garlic

2 tablespoons olive oil

2 tablespoons fresh lemon juice

1 tablespoon chia seeds

1 tablespoon roasted sunflower kernels

½ teaspoon ground cumin

½ teaspoon salt

10 baby carrots

¼ English cucumber, peeled and sliced

2 ribs celery, cut into sticks

In a food processor, combine the chickpeas, tahini, yogurt, garlic, oil, lemon juice, chia seeds, sunflower kernels, cumin, and salt. Process until smooth. Serve ¼-cup servings with the vegetables.

Nutrition per serving: 174 calories, 6 g protein, 13 g carbohydrates, 4 g fiber, 2 g sugar, 12 g fat, 1.5 g saturated fat, 356 mg sodium

Strawberry-Chia Yogurt

Shrink your waistline with two belly fat–fighting foods: chia and yogurt. Chia seeds begin to "gel" in wet ingredients; the longer you let this snack sit in the fridge, the more puddinglike it will become.

Makes 1 serving

1 cup low-fat plain Greek yogurt

½ cup sliced strawberries

1 teaspoon chia seeds

In a medium bowl, combine the yogurt, strawberries, and chia seeds. Refrigerate for 1 hour or more before serving.

Nutrition per serving: 235 calories, 27 g protein, 18 g carbohydrates, 3 g fiber, 14 g sugar, 6 g fat, 4 g saturated fat, 82 mg sodium

Apple and Peanut Butter Dippers

This simple, satiating snack combines fiber-rich apple with protein-filled peanut butter. Feel free to swap out the peanut butter for another natural nut butter.

Makes 1 serving

2 tablespoons natural smooth peanut butter

1 teaspoon hemp seeds

1 apple, cored and cut into wedges

In a small bowl, combine the peanut butter and hemp seeds. Serve the apple wedges with the peanut butter dip.

Nutrition per serving: 314 calories, 9 g protein, 33 g carbohydrates, 6 g fiber, 21 g sugar, 18 g fat, 2 g saturated fat, 122 mg sodium

Banana-Walnut Protein Bars

You could rip a bar out of a package, or you could take a few minutes to whip up these—which taste like legit banana bread.

Makes 16 servings

2 cups walnuts, ground until very fine in a blender or food processor

½ cup old-fashioned rolled oats

6 scoops vanilla protein powder (whey or pea)

¼ teaspoon baking powder

Pinch of salt

2 very ripe bananas, mashed

2 eggs

2 tablespoons unsalted butter, melted and cooled slightly

2–3 tablespoons water, as needed

1. Preheat the oven to 350°F. Coat an 11″ × 7″ nonstick baking pan with olive oil cooking spray.

2. In a large bowl, mix together the walnuts, oats, protein powder, baking powder, and salt. In a separate bowl, mix together the bananas, eggs, and butter. Pour into the walnut mixture, adding the water, if needed, to mix well.

3. Press the mixture into the prepared baking pan and bake for 12 minutes, or until a knife comes out clean from the sides of the pan (not the middle). It should be slightly underbaked in the middle. Allow to cool before cutting into 16 bars.

Nutrition per serving: 185 calories, 12 g protein, 8 g carbohydrates, 2 g fiber, 3 g sugar, 13 g fat, 2 g saturated fat, 45 mg sodium

Peanut Butter–Flax Fudge Bars

These no-bake bars have a rich toffeelike flavor. Whey protein makes them a great post-workout snack.

Makes 4 servings

⅔ cup ground flaxseeds

4 scoops chocolate whey protein isolate powder

¼ cup chunky natural peanut butter

¼ cup water

1. In a large bowl, mix together the flaxseeds, protein powder, peanut butter, and water. At first, it will seem like it's not enough water, but keep stirring; it will eventually become a sticky blob of dough. If necessary, add more water, 1 tablespoon at a time.

2. Divide the mixture into 4 equal portions. Put them onto separate pieces of plastic wrap, shaping each into a bar within the wrap. (It's easier to shape them by laying the plastic wrap along one side of a small casserole dish, pressing the dough into the natural shape of the dish.)

3. Put the bars into the refrigerator, or store them in the freezer. You can eat them chilled, frozen—or right out of the bowl if you're feeling impatient!

Nutrition per serving: 300 calories, 31 g protein, 10 g carbohydrates, 6 g fiber, 1.5 g sugar, 16 g fat, 2 g saturated fat, 121 mg sodium

Ricotta Cheese with Cinnamon and Berries

Toasty cinnamon and summer berries pair well with creamy ricotta in this sweet and savory snack.

Makes 1 serving

1 teaspoon ground cinnamon

½ cup part-skim ricotta cheese

¼ cup berries (blueberries, raspberries, or sliced strawberries)

Sprinkle the cinnamon over the ricotta cheese and top with the berries.

Nutrition per serving: 199 calories, 14 g protein, 14 g carbohydrates, 2 g fiber, 4 g sugar, 10 g fat, 6 g saturated fat, 156 mg sodium

Mini "Pizzas"

These petite pies strike the right balance between delicious and nutritious.

1 stick (about ¾ ounce) part-skim mozzarella string cheese

1 sprouted grain English muffin, split

¼ cup halved cherry tomatoes

½ teaspoon dried oregano

1. Preheat the broiler or toaster oven.

2. Shred the string cheese and cover each half of the muffin. Top with the tomatoes and oregano.

3. Set on a baking sheet and broil for 2 minutes, or until the cheese is melted and the tomatoes are slightly blistered. Serve.

Nutrition per serving: 247 calories, 16 g protein, 32 g carbohydrates, 6 g fiber, 1 g sugar, 7 g fat, 3.5 g saturated fat, 392 mg sodium

High-Fiber Berry Yogurt

I don't know about you, but I need a topping on my frozen yogurt *and* my regular yogurt. High-fiber cereal lends texture without added sugar.

Makes 1 serving

1 container (5.3 ounces) low-fat plain Greek yogurt

⅓ cup sprouted grain cereal

¼ cup blueberries

In a bowl, mix the yogurt with the cereal and top with the berries.

Nutrition per serving: 260 calories, 21 g protein, 38 g carbohydrates, 5 g fiber, 10 g sugar, 4 g fat, 2 g saturated fat, 183 mg sodium

Heavenly Deviled Eggs

My kids love Easter for the candy, but to me the holiday is all about deviled eggs. These use Greek yogurt instead of mayo.

Makes 1 serving

2 hard-cooked eggs

2 tablespoons low-fat plain Greek yogurt

1 teaspoon Dijon or yellow mustard

Pinch of salt

Pinch of ground black pepper

½ teaspoon chopped chives

Pinch of paprika

1. Slice the eggs in half lengthwise and carefully remove the yolks.

2. In a small bowl, mix together the yolks, yogurt, mustard, salt, and pepper.

3. Spoon the mixture into each egg white. Sprinkle with the chives and paprika.

Nutrition per serving: 185 calories, 16 g protein, 4 g carbohydrates, 0 g fiber, 2 g sugar, 11 g fat, 4 g saturated fat, 400 mg sodium

Curry Spiced Nuts

Okay, so these seasoned nuts technically take more than 30 minutes to prepare—they sit in a slow cooker for 1 to 2 hours—but they're worth the wait, and the recipe makes extra batches that you can divide into zip-top bags and snack on later.

Makes 16 servings (2 ounces each)

6 ounces raw cashews

6 ounces raw almonds

6 ounces raw pecan halves

3 tablespoons coconut oil, melted

4 teaspoons curry powder

2 teaspoons honey

½ teaspoon garlic powder

¼ teaspoon salt

¼ teaspoon ground red pepper

1. In a 6-quart slow cooker, stir together the cashews, almonds, pecans, coconut oil, curry powder, honey, garlic powder, salt, and ground red pepper.

2. Cover and cook on high, stirring occasionally, for 1½ to 2 hours, or until golden and crisp.

3. Transfer the nuts to a parchment-lined baking sheet and spread in an even layer to cool and dry. Transfer to an airtight container.

Nutrition per serving: 220 calories, 5 g protein, 8 g carbohydrates, 3 g fiber, 2 g sugar, 20 g fat, 4 g saturated fat, 62 mg sodium

SMOOTHIES

Smoothies are a good way to get in a variety of nutrients, and sweet fruit and protein powder make veggies more palatable. For each smoothie, combine all of the ingredients in a blender and process on medium-high speed until smooth and creamy. Add more ice to make it thicker, or add water to make it smoother. When a recipe calls for protein powder, choose whey or pea powder. Each recipe makes 1 serving.

Chocolate-Cherry Bliss

1 cup unsweetened chocolate almond milk (or water)

1 scoop chocolate protein powder

1 cup frozen dark sweet cherries

½ cup baby spinach

1 tablespoon ground flaxseeds

1 tablespoon cacao nibs

5 ice cubes

Nutrition per serving: 362 calories, 30 g protein, 40 g carbohydrates, 13 g fiber, 19 g sugar, 11 g fat, 3 g saturated fat, 255 mg sodium

Vanilla Pumpkin Pie

1 cup unsweetened vanilla almond milk (or water)

1 scoop vanilla protein powder

½ cup canned pumpkin

2 teaspoons honey

1 tablespoon ground flaxseeds

2 tablespoons walnuts

Pinch of ground cinnamon

Pinch of ground nutmeg

5 ice cubes

Nutrition per serving: 378 calories, 29 g protein, 30 g carbohydrates, 8 g fiber, 17 g sugar, 18 g fat, 2 g saturated fat, 242 mg sodium

Piña Colada

1 cup unsweetened coconut milk beverage or ⅓ cup unsweetened canned coconut milk + ⅔ cup water

1 scoop vanilla protein powder

½ cup fresh or canned and drained pineapple chunks

½ banana

5 ice cubes

Nutrition per serving: 264 calories, 25 g protein, 27 g carbohydrates, 3 g fiber, 16 g sugar, 7 g fat, 6 g saturated fat, 70 mg sodium

Strawberries and Cream

1 cup unsweetened vanilla almond milk

⅓ cup fresh or frozen strawberries

¼ cup old-fashioned rolled oats

1 scoop strawberries and cream protein powder or vanilla protein powder

2 tablespoons low-fat plain Greek yogurt

5 ice cubes

Nutrition per serving: 277 calories, 30 g protein, 23 g carbohydrates, 4 g fiber, 5 g sugar, 7 g fat, 1.5 g saturated fat, 244 mg sodium

Apple Pie in a Cup

1 cup unsweetened vanilla almond milk (or water)

1 apple, cored

2 tablespoons walnuts

1 scoop vanilla protein powder

½ teaspoon ground cinnamon

5 ice cubes

Nutrition per serving: 354 calories, 27 g protein, 32 g carbohydrates, 7 g fiber, 20 g sugar, 15 g fat, 2 g saturated fat, 235 mg sodium

Vanilla and Cinnamon Mocha Smoothie

1 cup unsweetened vanilla almond milk

1 scoop chocolate protein powder

1 heaping teaspoon instant coffee

½ teaspoon ground cinnamon

5 ice cubes

2 tablespoons almonds (optional)

Nutrition per serving: 167 calories, 24 g protein, 6 g carbohydrates, 2 g fiber, 1 g sugar, 5 g fat, 1 g saturated fat, 234 mg sodium

TREATS

High-Protein Brownies

These chocolaty brownies will hit the spot when you're craving a baked good. For an earthier, nuttier option, use buckwheat flour instead of oat flour.

Makes 9

1 cup oat flour

2 scoops chocolate whey protein powder

3 tablespoons unsweetened cocoa powder

2 tablespoons mini chocolate chips

½ teaspoon baking soda

¼ teaspoon salt

1 cup unsweetened applesauce

½ cup liquid egg whites (or 4 egg whites)

2 tablespoons chopped walnuts

1. Preheat the oven to 350°F. Coat a 9″ × 9″ baking pan with olive oil cooking spray.

2. In a medium bowl, mix together the flour, protein powder, cocoa powder, chocolate chips, baking soda, and salt.

3. Add the applesauce and egg whites, mixing gently until just combined. Pour the batter into the pan, smooth the top, and sprinkle with the walnuts.

4. Bake for 10 to 12 minutes, or until a wooden pick inserted into the center comes out with moist crumbs. Cool completely before cutting into 9 brownies.

Nutrition per serving: 116 calories, 9 g protein, 14 g carbohydrates, 2 g fiber, 4 g sugar, 4 g fat, 1 g saturated fat, 172 mg sodium

Carrot-Apple Oat Muffins

Have one of these fiber-filled, not-too-sweet muffins as a snack, or add one to your breakfast.

Makes 6

¾ cup liquid egg whites (or 6 egg whites)

1 egg

1 tablespoon maple syrup

1 teaspoon vanilla extract

2 cups old-fashioned rolled oats

¼ cup oat bran

⅓ cup grated carrot

¼ cup chopped tart green apple

1 teaspoon ground cinnamon

½ teaspoon salt

¼ teaspoon ground nutmeg

1. Preheat the oven to 350°F. Line a 6-cup muffin pan with paper liners.

2. In a large bowl, combine the egg whites, egg, syrup, and vanilla and stir until well mixed. Add the oats, oat bran, carrot, apple, cinnamon, salt, and nutmeg and mix until just combined.

3. Divide the batter among the muffin cups and bake for 15 to 20 minutes, or until the tops are brown and a wooden pick inserted into one comes out clean. Cool in the pan for 5 minutes before removing the muffins to a rack to cool.

Nutrition per serving: 155 calories, 8 g protein, 25 g carbohydrates, 4 g fiber, 4 g sugar, 3 g fat, 0.5 g saturated fat, 237 mg sodium

Hemp Seed Cookies

The star ingredient in these light, crisp cookies is hemp, a complete protein that contains omega-3s, 6s, and 9s; fiber; and chlorophyll (an important source of antioxidants). You can find hemp seeds (sometimes referred to as hulled hemp hearts) in the natural foods section of your grocery store.

Makes 16 (8 servings)

1 egg

6 tablespoons coconut oil, melted and cooled slightly

⅓ cup packed brown sugar

1 cup hemp seeds

⅓ cup white or brown rice flour

¼ cup oat bran or oat flour

2 teaspoons ground cinnamon

1. Preheat the oven to 350°F. Lightly coat a baking sheet with olive oil cooking spray or line it with parchment paper.

2. In a medium bowl, lightly whisk the egg. Mix in the oil and sugar. In a separate bowl, mix together the hemp seeds, rice flour, oat bran or oat flour, and cinnamon. Add the wet ingredients to the dry and mix until a thick dough forms.

3. Drop 16 Ping-Pong-ball-size dollops of dough on the baking sheet and bake for 12 minutes, or until brown around the edges. Cool on the baking sheet for 1 minute before transferring the cookies to a rack to cool.

Nutrition per serving: 279 calories, 8 g protein, 20 g carbohydrates, 1 g fiber, 10 g sugar, 19 g fat, 10 g saturated fat, 12 mg sodium

Four-Ingredient Peanut Butter Cookies

These moist cookies have extra peanut butter flavor—and no flour. If you'd like to amp up the protein, enjoy a cookie with $\frac{1}{4}$ cup of low-fat plain Greek yogurt.

Makes about 18

1 cup natural peanut butter

1 cup packed brown sugar

1 egg

1 teaspoon vanilla extract

1. Place a rack in the lower third of the oven. Preheat the oven to 350°F.

2. In a medium bowl, add the peanut butter, sugar, egg, and vanilla. With an electric mixer, beat the mixture until well combined.

3. On an ungreased baking sheet, set tablespoons of the mixture 1" apart. Flatten the scoops with the tines of a fork, making a crisscross pattern on the cookies.

4. Bake for 10 minutes, or until golden brown around the edges.

5. Cool on the baking sheet for 1 minute before transferring the cookies to a rack to cool completely.

Nutrition per serving: 140 calories, 3 g protein (with Greek yogurt, 10 g), 15 g carbohydrates, 1 g fiber, 13 g sugar, 7 g fat, 1 g saturated fat, 61 mg sodium

"I Did It!"

NAME: Sarah DeArmond

AGE: **30**

HOMETOWN: **Calera, Alabama**

BEFORE WEIGHT: **200**

AFTER WEIGHT: **100**

SARAH'S STORY: As a kid, Sarah was teased about her weight—for being too skinny! "My metabolism must have been great, because I got away with eating fattening foods like mashed potatoes and fried chicken," she says. Taking dance classes for 10 years helped, but once Sarah hit college, a lack of physical activity and her fast-food habit took its toll. She packed on 15 pounds—and added more weight to her frame after she got hitched in 2009. Rather than cooking, "we just microwaved pizzas or cheesy pastas every night," she says.

WAKE-UP CALL: Sarah noticed her size 14 pants were getting tight, and then someone asked her when she was due—and she wasn't pregnant!

SUCCESS SECRETS: In the spring of 2013, Sarah started overhauling her diet. She searched Pinterest for recipes featuring lean protein like turkey and chicken and cooked those instead of microwaving frozen dinners. She learned to lower the fat content of her meals—without sacrificing flavor—by using spices. The change was instantaneous: "I felt so much better that I honestly didn't even miss my greasy go-to foods," she says. She also started speed walking 2 miles a day around her hilly neighborhood—and her weight started dropping. When the scale got stuck, she blasted through the plateau by adding half-hour strength training sessions to her schedule. She worked her way up to hoisting 10-pound weights and stepped up her cardio routine to 5 miles of daily power walking. Now Sarah is a trim and healthy 100 pounds. "I had no idea that I would end up losing 100 pounds," she says. "This has been such a blessing."

Chocolate–Almond Butter Energy Balls

Eat one of these big balls, which contain whey powder, after a workout to recharge your batteries.

Makes 10

1 cup old-fashioned rolled oats

1 cup unsweetened shredded coconut

½ cup natural almond butter

½ cup semisweet chocolate chips

⅓ cup honey

2 scoops vanilla whey protein powder

1. In a medium bowl, combine the oats, coconut, almond butter, chocolate chips, honey, and protein powder. Mix until well blended and doughlike.

2. Form into 10 golf-ball-size balls, set on a plate, and refrigerate for 30 minutes, or until firm. Store in the refrigerator in an airtight container for up to 2 weeks.

Nutrition per serving: 271 calories, 10 g protein, 25 g carbohydrates, 4 g fiber, 15 g sugar, 16 g fat, 7.5 g saturated fat, 42 mg sodium

9

The TIAO Workout

The Take It All Off Workout is a calorie-burning, muscle-building, metabolism-revving plan designed to fit into a busy lifestyle. The program can be done at home, with minimal equipment, and offers simple, effective routines that will help make fitness a lifelong habit. It's broken down into three 2-month phases, which build upon each other so you continue to challenge your body. Just when one phase is becoming a cinch (or you start plateauing), it's time to move on to the next phase! The goal of the plan is to melt away fat with cardio, which incinerates calories, and strength training, which boosts growth hormone and testosterone (these hormones help muscles burn fat for energy). The strength moves are super effective because they target several different muscle groups at once, which increases metabolism, and each phase kicks off with moves specifically designed to blast belly flab.

You'll be exercising 6 days a week. This may sound like a lot, but that's what it takes to shed pounds, and it's also the number of days recommended by the American College of Sports Medicine (ACSM). Your off day should be an "active rest" day, meaning do something low key like walking, yoga, gardening, golfing, or whatever else you find fun and relaxing. The good news is that you only have to work out for 30 minutes a day (although there is an option in each phase to go longer for faster results), and you only need the following equipment.

- Loop-style resistance bands—no handles (order them online at resistancebandtraining.com or find them at sporting goods stores or retail outlets such as Target)
- A pair of 8- to 12-pound dumbbells
- A step (or stair)
- Furniture sliders (you can buy them at any hardware store)
- A take-no-prisoners attitude!

WARMUP

Before you start any phase of this routine, loosen up by doing 5 minutes of light walking, running, or biking. Then try these dynamic warmup exercises, which will mobilize and activate your muscles, preventing injury. Do 10 reps of each, unless otherwise noted. (If you don't have time to do all of the moves, just do as many as you can.)

ANKLE ROCKERS

Get down into Downward Dog pose (bring your hands to the floor and walk out into an inverted V shape). Place one foot behind the other so your toes are resting on the heel of the other foot and the ball of only one foot is touching the floor. Raise your heel off the ground until you're on your toes. Let your heel come back down to the ground. That's 1 rep. Repeat 10 times on one foot and 10 times on the other. If this is too hard, pedal your legs out, pushing one knee forward at a time while keeping both feet on the ground.

SPIDERMAN LUNGE WITH ARM REACH

From Downward Dog, step your right foot forward and place it as close to your right hand as possible. Lean forward at your hips, and keep your left hand on the floor while you reach your right hand and arm toward the ceiling. Return to Downward Dog. That's 1 rep. Repeat with your left side.

PRONE BLACKBURNS

Lie facedown on the floor and place your hands on the small of your back (palms facing out), arms bent. Squeeze your shoulder blades together to bring your elbows off the floor. Sweep your arms up and out to the sides to a Y position (so each arm is on either side of your head). Return your hands to your back.

INCHWORM WALKOUTS

Standing with your legs straight, bend over at the hips and touch the floor with your hands. (If you can't reach the floor with your legs straight, bend your knees a little). Keeping your legs straight, walk your hands forward into a plank position. Then walk your hands back to your feet, keeping your legs as straight as possible, and stand up. That's 1 rep.

LOW SIDE-TO-SIDE LUNGES

Stand with your feet set about twice shoulder-width apart, feet facing straight ahead. Place your hands in a prayer position. Shift your weight over to your right leg and bend your right knee, keeping your knee behind your toes, butt pushed back. Your lower right leg should be nearly perpendicular to the floor; your left foot should remain flat on the floor and your left leg as straight as possible. Without raising yourself back up to the starting position (if you can), reverse the movement to the left. That's 1 rep.

PRISONER SQUATS

Standing tall, clasp your hands behind your head, keeping your chest high and abs braced. Drop your hips back and shift your weight onto your heels until you're in a squatting position. Squeeze your glutes to stand back up.

JUMPING JACKS

You know how to do these, so I won't bore you with directions. But here are a couple of tips: Stay on your toes the whole time, and if you can't clap your hands over your head, simply reach your fingertips toward each other over your head, palms facing forward. Do 30 of them.

FIVE WAYS TO PREVENT INJURY

YOU CAN'T GET FIT LYING ON THE COUCH WITH A BAG OF FROZEN PEAS DRAPED OVER YOUR ANKLE. OUCH-PROOF YOUR ROUTINE WITH THESE TIPS.

1. Warm Up

The research on stretching is conflicting, but most experts recommend moving your joints and muscles pre-workout to help ward off pulls, sprains, and tears. Do a mix of static stretching and dynamic exercises (see examples in the warmup), and when you're lifting weights, start by using lighter dumbbells, and then move on to heavier ones to prevent shocking your muscles.

2. Use Good Form

Following the directions outlined in this chapter will help you maintain good form throughout each exercise. When trying new routines, it's not a bad idea to invest in a few sessions with a trainer. (In lieu of that, ask a trainer on the gym floor how to use a piece of equipment if you have no clue what you're doing.) A few tips that will automatically help you keep proper form through most moves: Look straight ahead (not down or up); keep your abs contracted and your back straight; and make sure your knees are in line with your second toe (not way in front of the second toe), which will help ward off knee injuries.

3. Take It Slow

Whipping through lifting exercises can strain your joints and cause you to break form. To slow yourself down, raise the weight to a count of 3 and lower it to a count of 3.

4. Don't Overdo It

Going balls to the wall is good—unless your body isn't ready for it. It's like taking a test without studying first! The moves in Phase 1 will help prepare your muscles to go hard in later phases, minimizing injury. Examples of pushing too hard include being sore for longer than 3 days, loss of appetite, or inability to sleep.

5. Switch It Up

When you lift, you have to practice the moves to do them correctly. But doing the same cardio workout day in and day out can lead to over-use injuries and muscle imbalances (for example, if you do a routine that targets your quads and neglects your hamstrings, there's a chance you are putting your knees at risk). Mix up your cardio routine so you're not doing the same type of exercises on all of your cardio days.

Phase 1

Phase 1 of the Take It All Off Workout is designed for women who haven't exercised regularly for at least a year. (If you've already been working up a sweat on a regular basis, you can skip to Phase 2.) Phase 1 includes 3 days of strength training and 3 days of cardio, and it will help you build the muscle strength and cardiovascular endurance necessary to tackle the challenging, fat-torching phases that come later in the program.

STRENGTH TRAINING MOVES

Here are the moves you will be doing in Phase 1. The charts on pages 176 to 178 explain exactly how many reps to do for each exercise. Some of these exercises call for continuous-loop resistance bands. You will find that bands come in four levels of resistance; the wider and heavier the band, the more resistance. Play around with the bands until you figure out which one gives you the right amount of resistance for each move (for example, you'll want a lighter band for moves like overhead presses and a heavier one for things like deadlifts). As you get stronger, upgrade to a heavier band. (A resistance band should be heavy enough to challenge your body, but not so heavy that it causes sharp pain or excessive soreness for more than 3 days.) Here are the moves in the order they appear in the Phase 1 Routine.

FOREARM FRONT-BODY PLANK

Start to get into a pushup position, but bend your elbows and rest your weight on your forearms instead of your hands. (Your body should form a straight line from your head to your ankles. Make sure your butt is down!) Contract your abs as if you were about to be punched in the gut, and hold the position for 10 to 30 seconds.

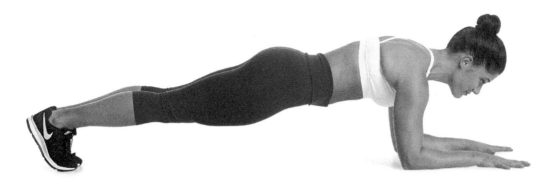

SIDE-BODY PLANK

Lie on your left side with your legs straight. Prop your upper body up on your left elbow and forearm, and brace your abs. (If that's too tough, bend your left knee 90 degrees.) Raise your hips until your body forms a straight line from your ankles to your shoulders, and hold the position for 10 to 30 seconds; lower your hips back down to the ground. Repeat on your right side.

ECCENTRIC PUSHUP WITH KNEE-ASSIST UP

Get down into a pushup position with your arms and legs completely straight. (Your body should form a straight line from your head to your ankles.) Squeeze your glutes, brace your abs, and very slowly, to a count of 4, lower your body until your chest *nearly* touches the floor. Pause, and then drop your knees to the floor and push your body back up (not pictured). If you don't have the strength to do this yet, place your hands on a table or bench so that they're slightly wider than shoulder-width apart. (The higher the table, the easier it will be.) Lower your body slowly to a count of 4, pause, and then step one foot forward to push your body back to the starting position as quickly as possible.

SEATED RESISTANCE BAND ROW

Sit on the floor with your legs extended straight out in front of you. Hook the resistance band around your feet. To make it even harder, hook both sides of the resistance band behind the soles of your feet, and grab an end with each hand. Keeping your chest high and abs tight, pull the band toward your belly, squeezing your shoulder blades together. Release the tension on the band, straightening your arms, and return the band to the starting position.

RESISTANCE BAND SQUAT

Stand with your feet shoulder-width apart, brace your abs, and hold your arms straight out in front of you at shoulder level. Lower your body, by bending your knees and pushing your hips back until your quads are parallel to the floor. (Keep your weight on your heels, not your toes, to ensure your knees stay in line with your second toe.) Pause, and then push your body back up to the starting position. Once you've mastered the bodyweight squat, add a resistance band: Loop one end of a band under your feet and place the other end across the front and top of your shoulders, crossing your arms in front of you and raising them until they are parallel to the floor to prevent the band from falling off.

SINGLE LEG STEPUP

Stand in front of a riser, bench, table, or step, and place your left foot firmly on the surface. The surface should be high enough so that your knee is bent at a 90-degree angle—no higher! Keep your abs tight, pull your shoulders back, and press your left heel into the riser or bench and push your body up until your left leg is straight and you are standing tall. The right foot does not touch the riser. Squeeze your glutes; then lower your body back down until your right foot touches the floor. Your left foot will remain on the step until you complete all reps. Then switch legs to work the other side.

SUPINE HIP EXTENSION

Lie on your back with your knees bent and your feet flat on the floor. Arms should be at your sides, palms facing down. Squeeze your glutes to raise your hips off the floor so your body forms a straight line from your shoulders to your knees. (Make sure you push against the floor with your heels, not your toes, and don't arch your back.) Your arms will stay on the floor. Relax your glutes to return your lower body back to the starting position. Want to up the intensity? Do the move with a dumbbell resting on your hips, raising them slowly so the dumbbell stays in place.

BEAR HOLD

Get down on your hands and knees with your palms flat on the floor and shoulder-width apart. Without allowing your lower back to rise or round, brace your abs as if you were about to be punched in the gut. Flex your toes and lift your knees off the ground 1 to 2 inches; keep your knees elevated for 10 to 30 seconds, breathing deeply throughout the exercise. (Your body will look like a bear in this position.) Keep your arms tight to your sides while holding this move, which forces your core to work harder. Return your knees to the ground.

CRAB HIP HOLD

Sit with your knees bent, feet flat on the floor, and place your hands on the floor about 8 inches behind your butt, with your fingers facing your body. Squeeze your glutes and brace your abs to lift your hips up so that your body forms a straight line from your knees to your shoulders. Look up at the ceiling and hold the position for 10 to 30 seconds while keeping your glutes tight. Relax your glutes to return to the starting position.

RESISTANCE BAND OVERHEAD PRESS

Stand tall with your feet shoulder-width apart, core tight, and knees slightly bent. Loop a resistance band under your feet, and hold the other end in front of your shoulders, palms facing out. Push the band straight overhead. Your arms should be completely straight and the band should be directly above your shoulders. Pause, and then slowly lower the band back to the starting position.

RESISTANCE BAND UPRIGHT ROW
WITH SIDE STEP

Stand with your feet shoulder-width apart and your knees slightly bent. Loop a resistance band under your feet, and grab the other end of the band with each hand. Your arms will be hanging straight down in front of your body as you hold the band. In one movement, pull the band up to your chest, driving your elbows to the ceiling, and at the same time, step your right foot out to the side, keeping your core engaged. Pause, and then lower the band and step your foot back to the starting position. Repeat on the opposite side.

RESISTANCE BAND DEADLIFT

These deadlifts are much more "back friendly" than those that use barbells. Using a band will help you keep your core tight and your glutes engaged, preventing injury. Stand with your feet wider than shoulder-width apart. Bend your knees and push your hips back to squat down. Loop a band around each foot so you are stepping on one side of the band and the other side is lying across the laces of your sneakers. Grab the middle of the band with your hands. To make it harder, grab both sides of the band. Hands should be about shoulder-width apart, with palms facing you. Keeping your arms tight to your sides (this is very important!), hold on to the band tightly as you stand back up, pushing through with your glutes and keeping your abs tight. Get back down into a squat and repeat.

RESISTANCE BAND GOOD MORNING

While standing, bend over by pushing your hips back and keeping your legs straight. (Your chest should be parallel to the floor.) Loop one end of a resistance band under your feet, and then place the other behind your neck. Hold on to the band lightly in front of your shoulders. Keeping your core tight, squeeze your glutes to push your hips forward and stand up. Return back to the starting position. The purpose of this movement is to strengthen your spinal erector muscles (the muscles on either side of your spine), along with your hamstrings and glutes. This move is especially tough; don't move on to a heavier band until you've totally mastered the exercise. If you experience any low-back pain, skip this move.

RESISTANCE BAND
OVERHEAD TRICEPS EXTENSION

Stand up straight and loop one side of a resistance band under your right foot. Bring the band behind your body with both hands and pull it up toward your head, palms facing the ceiling and elbows pointing up. At the same time, step forward with your left foot. Extend your arms to pull the band up toward the ceiling, pause, and then slowly lower the band back behind your head. When you do this move in Phases 2 and 3, pause with your arms bent at 90 degrees behind your head and quickly pulse the band up and down for 10 seconds before returning to the starting position.

RESISTANCE BAND BICEPS CURL

Standing with your feet shoulder-width apart and knees slightly bent, loop one side of a resistance band underneath your feet. Grasp the other side of the band with both hands and hold it in front of your thighs, palms facing out. Brace your core and curl the band toward your chest. Pause, and then slowly lower the band to the starting position. When you do this move in Phases 2 and 3, pause with your arms bent at 90 degrees in front of your body and quickly pulse the band up and down for 10 seconds before returning to the starting position.

SLOW MOUNTAIN CLIMBER

Get down into a pushup position with your arms completely straight. (Your body should form a straight line from your head to your ankles.) Brace your core, lift your right foot off the floor, and then slowly pull your knee toward your abdomen so it forms a 90-degree angle with your hips. Hold for 1 to 3 seconds, breathing deeply. Return your foot to the starting position. Do 10, and then do 10 more with your other knee.

AB SQUIRMS

Lie on your back with your knees bent and feet flat on the floor, arms at your sides. Bracing your core, reach your right hand to your right heel, flexing your torso to one side. That's 1 rep. Repeat on the left side, reaching your left hand to your left heel.

RESISTANCE BAND SQUAT TO CHEST PRESS

Loop both sides of a band behind your upper back (imagine you are wrapping a blanket around yourself). Bring each end under your arms so your hands are in front of your chest; your fists will be facing each other as you hold the band. Push your hips back and bend at the knees to squat down. Push back up to a standing position while pressing the band out in front of you until your arms are straight (or as straight as you can get them). Bend your arms at the elbows to return the band close to your chest.

RESISTANCE BAND BENT-OVER ROW

Bend over at the waist, knees slightly bent, abs contracted, and chest forward. Loop both sides of a resistance band underneath your feet. Grasp an end with each hand, keeping your arms straight and hanging below your chest. Bend your arms at the elbows and squeeze your shoulder blades together to make a rowing motion. Pull the band toward your chest, squeezing tight between your shoulder blades (but do not shrug!). Pause, and then lower the band back to the starting position by straightening your arms.

RESISTANCE BAND SPLIT SQUAT

Stand with your feet hip-width apart. Loop one side of a resistance band under your right foot and rest the other side across your shoulders. The band should sit on your shoulders. Cross your arms and raise them so they are parallel to the floor to hold the band in place. Step back with your left foot so just your toes are touching the floor. Keeping your torso straight, bend your right knee to lower your body toward the floor until your left knee is parallel with the floor, keeping your knee behind your toes. Pause, and then squeeze your glutes and push back up to the starting position. That's 1 rep. Do 8 to 12 reps and then switch legs.

FROG HIP THRUST PUMPS

Lie on your back, bend your knees, and press the soles of your feet together. Your arms, bent at the elbow, will be on the floor at your sides. Squeezing your glutes and keeping your abs tight, quickly raise your hips as high as you can in the air. Lower them quickly to the floor—without quite touching the floor—and then quickly raise them back up again. That's 1 rep.

"I Did It!"

KRYSTAL'S STORY: While working as an Internal Revenue specialist, Krystal hit the drive-thru 5 nights a week. Then the stress of planning her upcoming nuptials drove her to eat even more—to the point where she had to buy a size 18 wedding dress. "I was in denial and avoided scales, cameras, and mirrors," she recalls.

NAME: **Krystal Sanders**
AGE: **32**
HOMETOWN: **Spring, Texas**
BEFORE WEIGHT: **185**
AFTER WEIGHT: **130**

WAKE-UP CALL: When Krystal's wedding pictures arrived in October 2008, she didn't want anyone to see them. "I looked at the pictures alone and cried," she says. "It was a reality punch in the face. I was embarrassed that I'd let myself get that large."

SUCCESS SECRETS: Krystal cleaned out her pantry and fridge, tossing all chips, frozen pizza, and other junk foods. Instead of eating out, she started cooking healthier versions of her favorite restaurant foods, eating more veggies, and measuring portions. "It was an eye-opener to see the difference between what I would normally eat and what the serving size was," she says. Krystal began jogging on her treadmill for 30 minutes six times a week, and over the next year, she added DVD strength workouts, cut out soda and processed foods—and reached her goal of 130 pounds. "I couldn't believe it. I thought maybe the scale was broken," says Krystal. Now she runs with her 2-year-old son in the stroller and bikes and hikes with her husband.

PHASE 1 ROUTINE

You will be strength training 3 days a week. Complete the first 3-day routine on Weeks 1, 2, 5, and 6; complete the second 3-day routine on Weeks 3, 4, 7, and 8. Rest for 30 to 60 seconds after each exercise. Opt for the lower number of sets if you want to keep your workout at 30 minutes—if you feel up to it and have extra time, do the max number of sets suggested for each move, which should take you 45 to 50 minutes. On non-strength-training days, you will do cardio, which you will learn about next.

Weeks 1, 2, 5, 6   DAY 1

EXERCISE	SETS	REPS
Forearm Front-Body Plank	1–2	10–30 seconds
Side-Body Plank	1–2	10–30 seconds
Eccentric Pushup	2–3	8–10
Seated Resistance Band Row	2–3	10–12
Resistance Band Squat	2–3	10–12
Stepup	2–3	8–10 each leg
Supine Hip Extension	2–3	15–20

DAY 2

EXERCISE	SETS	REPS
Bear Hold	1–2	10–30 seconds
Crab Hip Hold	1–2	10–30 seconds
Resistance Band Overhead Press	2–3	10–12
Resistance Band Upright Row with Side Step	2–3	10–12 each leg
Resistance Band Deadlift	2–3	10–12
Resistance Band Good Morning	2–3	10–12
Resistance Band Overhead Triceps Extension	2–3	12–15
Resistance Band Biceps Curl	2–3	12–15

DAY 3

EXERCISE	SETS	REPS
Slow Mountain Climber	2	10 each knee (3-second hold)
Ab Squirms	2	30 seconds
Resistance Band Squat to Chest Press	2–3	10–12
Resistance Band Bent-Over Row	2–3	10–12
Resistance Band Split Squat	2–3	8–12 each leg
Frog Hip Thrust Pumps	2–3	20–30

Weeks 3, 4, 7, 8

DAY 1

EXERCISE	SETS	REPS
Slow Mountain Climber	2	10 each knee (3-second hold)
Ab Squirms	2	30 seconds
Eccentric Pushup	2–3	8–10
Seated Resistance Band Row	2–3	10–12
Stepup	2–3	8–10 each leg
Supine Hip Extension	2–3	15–20

DAY 2

EXERCISE	SETS	REPS
Forearm Front-Body Plank	1–2	10–30 seconds
Side-Body Plank	1–2	10–30 seconds
Resistance Band Squat to Chest Press	2–3	10–12
Resistance Band Bent-Over Row	2–3	10–12
Resistance Band Deadlift	2–3	10–12
Resistance Band Good Morning	2–3	10–12
Resistance Band Overhead Triceps Extension	2–3	12–15
Resistance Band Biceps Curl	2–3	12–15

(continued)

PHASE 1 ROUTINE (cont.)

DAY 3

EXERCISE	SETS	REPS
Bear Hold	1–2	10–30 seconds
Crab Hip Hold	1–2	10–30 seconds
Resistance Band Overhead Press	2–3	10–12
Resistance Band Upright Row with Side Step	2–3	10–12 each leg
Resistance Band Split Squat	2–3	8–10 each leg
Frog Hip Thrust Pumps	2–3	20–30

EXTRA CREDIT

If you have time and energy to burn after your strength sessions, tack on this "finisher," which keeps you moving at a fast pace to get your heart rate up and torch extra calories. Do each of the following exercises for 30 seconds with no rest in between. Then rest for 30 seconds after all four moves have been completed in succession. Repeat two to four more times.

SPEED SKATERS

Stand with your feet shoulder-width apart. Bend your knees and push your hips back to lower your body 8 to 10 inches. Lean forward until your shoulders are above your knees and your arms are hanging straight down. Pushing through your left foot, lightly hop over to the right, swinging your arms to the right to help propel you, landing softly on your right foot, knee bent. Depending on how stable you feel, tap your left foot or keep it elevated once you land. Pause, and then push through your right foot to hop back to where your left foot was. Make sure you keep your core tight and knees soft throughout the move. Each time your foot makes contact with the ground is 1 rep. The wider and faster you hop, the more difficult the exercise will be.

STEP BACK, STAND UP BURPEES

Stand with your feet wider than shoulder-width apart and your abs tight. In one quick motion, squat down, place your hands on the floor, and jump your feet back behind your hands so that you are now in a high plank position. Pause, jump your feet back to where your hands are, and then stand up by squeezing your glutes. That's 1 rep.

HIGH PLANK JACKS

Get down into a high plank position, arms straight with elbows slightly bent. Brace your abs and squeeze your glutes. In one quick movement, jump your feet out wide and then jump them back in together so that you did a jumping jack in a plank position. That's 1 rep.

AB BICYCLES

Lie on your back with your knees bent, feet flat on the floor. Clasp your fingers behind your head, lifting your head slightly off the floor, pointing your elbows toward your knees. Raise your feet up off the floor so that your knees are bent at 90 degrees. Contracting your abs, reach your left elbow toward your right knee while extending your left leg straight out. Then return to the starting position. That's 1 rep. Repeat with the right elbow and left knee. Throughout the move, make sure your lower back maintains contact with the floor and your abs stay contracted.

CARDIO

In Phase 1, you will be doing cardio 3 days a week, on the days you are not strength training. To give your muscles a chance to recover, try to alternate days of cardio with days of strength training. (In other words, strength train on Monday, do cardio Tuesday, strength train on Wednesday, do cardio on Thursday, strength train Friday, and do cardio on Saturday.) Don't worry—no one expects you to be running a 10-K just yet. In Phase 1, the objective is to get you used to exercising at a sustained effort. Intervals (brief periods of intense exercise) will be added in later phases of the program; for now, just focus on getting your heart rate up to a point where it is tough to carry on a conversation—and on working out for a full 30 minutes. (That said, if you're crunched for time or 30 minutes feels too tough, it's totally fine to break your cardio workout into two 15-minute sessions.) Some good options include brisk walking, jogging, hiking, swimming, or bike riding—and classes like beginner boot camp, boxing, spinning, or dance. Sports like soccer, basketball, volleyball, and tennis count, too! Here is an example routine.

Week 1

DAY 1 Jog at a comfortable pace for 30 minutes.

DAY 2 Go for a half-hour hike.

DAY 3 Take a spin class or beginner boot camp class.

Week 2

DAY 1 Work out on an elliptical or stationary bike for 30 minutes.

DAY 2 Take a brisk 30-minute walk.

DAY 3 Play a sport like tennis, soccer, or basketball (for at least half an hour).

STRETCHING

We all get tempted to skip this part, but it's important to cool down your muscles post-workout to prevent injury and boost flexibility (it's the exercise equivalent of slowing down before a red light instead of suddenly slamming on the brakes). You don't have to stretch every day (the ACSM recommends limbering up two or three times a week). Hold each of the following moves for 10 to 30 seconds, and repeat each one two to four times.

SEATED BUTTERFLY STRETCH

Sit on the floor with your back straight and your knees bent and out to each side, the bottoms of your feet pressed together. Slowly lean forward until you feel a stretch in your inner thighs, hips, and low back. Hold, gently breathing in and out, for 10 to 30 seconds.

SEATED FIGURE-FOUR GLUTE STRETCH

Sit with your knees bent, feet flat on the floor. Lean back slightly with your hands on the floor behind you, fingers facing your body. Bend and cross one leg over the top of your opposite knee to form a number 4 shape with your legs. Lean toward your legs until you feel a slight stretch in your glute and hip. Hold for 10 to 30 seconds. Repeat with the other leg.

SEATED HAMSTRING STRETCH

Sit tall on the floor with your legs extended straight out in front of
you, feet relaxed, toes pointing up to the ceiling. Maintaining your
posture, slowly lean forward, reaching for your feet until you feel a
stretch in your hamstrings. Hold for 10 to 30 seconds.

DOWNWARD DOG

Get down on all fours and place your hands on the floor so that they're slightly wider than shoulder-width apart, arms straight. Straighten your legs until your body forms an inverted V shape from head to butt to ankles. (Your feet should be flat on the floor—or as close to flat as you can get them.) Push through your arms to press your chest toward your legs. This will stretch your chest and shoulders, as well as your hips and hamstrings. Hold for 10 to 30 seconds.

STANDING WIDE-ARM CHEST STRETCH

Stand tall and raise your arms directly out to your sides, parallel to the floor, palms facing forward. Reach out to your sides as wide as you can, through your fingers. Hold for 10 to 30 seconds.

GENTLE SIDE NECK STRETCH

Reach your left arm up and over your head and lightly grasp your right earlobe with your left hand. Gently pull your head toward your left shoulder until you feel a slight stretch on the right side of your neck. Hold, breathing in and out, for 10 to 30 seconds. Repeat on the other side.

Phase 2

Now you're ready to start the serious slimming and strengthening! Phase 2 follows a similar schedule as Phase 1—3 days of strength and 3 days of cardio for a period of 2 months—but it's more intense. Ideally, you will do a day of strength training followed by a day of cardio throughout the week, as you did in Phase 1.

For the strength training workout, the moves are divided into "supersets," meaning you perform one exercise and then immediately bang out the next one without resting in between the two moves. The lack of rest jacks up your heart rate, increasing your calorie burn. The cardio has also been pumped up to include periods of near-max effort followed by periods of rest, which research has shown burns through your body's abdominal fat stores, leading to a smaller waistline. You will recognize some of the moves from Phase 1 (the new ones follow), and warm up and cool down just as you did in Phase 1. Good luck—you can do it!

STRENGTH TRAINING MOVES

FOREARM FRONT-BODY PLANK WITH ALTERNATING TOE LIFTS

Get down into a forearm plank position, and tighten your abs and glutes. Slightly lift your right foot off the floor, and point your toes away from your body. Then lower your foot back to the floor, resting on your toes, and repeat with your left foot. Don't let your shoulders round or hips sag while you perform this exercise. Each toe lift is 1 rep.

BEAR CRAWL

Start in the Bear Hold position (page 161) with your abs tight and knees 1 to 2 inches off the ground. Simultaneously move your right hand and your left foot forward to begin the crawl; repeat this motion with your left hand and right leg, still keeping your knees 1 to 2 inches from the ground. Make sure your core stays tight, and don't let your body rock side to side as you crawl.

SUPINE HIP EXTENSION WITH MARCHING

Follow the Supine Hip Extension instructions from Phase 1 (page 160), but at the top of the movement, lift one knee to your abdomen, keeping your glutes tight, and then lower your foot back to the floor. Repeat this movement with the other leg, and continue to alternate back and forth. Each leg lift is 1 rep.

HIGH PLANK SHOULDER TAPS

Get down into a pushup position, so your body forms a straight line from your head to your ankles, with your legs spread slightly wider than shoulder-width apart. Squeeze your glutes and brace your abs. Making sure not to rock your hips, pick your right hand off the floor and tap your left shoulder; return your hand to the starting position. That's 1 rep. Repeat with your left hand.

SUPINE LEG LOWERS

Lie on your back with your legs extended straight up in the air (so they are perpendicular to the floor). Your head and neck will remain on the floor for this entire move. Place your hands under your butt, palms down, and brace your abs. Slowly lower both legs toward the floor (without quite touching it). As soon as you feel your lower back rounding off the floor, squeeze your abs to bring your legs back up to the starting position. If this bothers your lower back, only lower one leg at a time.

PUSHUP

Get down on all fours, and place your hands on the floor so that they're slightly wider than in line with your shoulders. If you can't support your body weight completely, place your hands on a coffee table or bench. Straighten your legs with your weight on your toes. Your body should form a straight line from your head to your ankles. Squeeze your glutes and brace your abs as you lower your body until your chest nearly touches the floor (or table). Pause at the bottom and then push your body back to the starting position as quickly as possible.

WALKING LUNGES

Stand with your feet shoulder-width apart, abs tight, chest up, and hands on your hips. Take a large step forward with your right foot. Sink your body toward the floor, bending your left knee enough so that your right knee doesn't pass your toes. Your knees should both be bent at 90 degrees. Then take a big step forward with your left foot, so your left foot is now far in front of your right. Do 10 to 15 steps with each leg. To make it harder, hold dumbbells at your sides while you perform the move.

SLIDER SUPINE HAMSTRING CURL

Lie on your back with your knees bent and each heel resting on top of a slider. Squeeze your glutes to raise your hips off the floor so your body forms a straight line from your shoulders to your knees. Slowly push your heels into the sliders to move your feet away from your body, controlling the movement with your hamstrings and glutes, until you feel a gentle stretch in the backs of your legs. Then, contracting your hamstrings and glutes, pull the sliders back in toward your butt, keeping your hips high and abs braced. That's 1 rep.

RESISTANCE BAND SQUAT
TO OVERHEAD PRESS

Follow the directions for the Resistance Band Overhead Press in Phase 1 (page 163). But this time, when you bring the band back down to your shoulders after pressing it overhead, you will also push your hips back and bend at the knees into a squat position, keeping the band in front of your body. As you stand back up from the squat, you will simultaneously push the band above your head again for another overhead press. That's 1 rep.

PHASE 2 ROUTINE

If you see A and B following the exercise number, this means you will perform exercise A, immediately followed by exercise B, then rest for 1 to 2 minutes and repeat for the desired amount of sets (for certain moves you have a choice of how many sets you want to do—go for the extra set for faster results). If you're having trouble cranking out some of these supersets, you can revert back to the earlier Phase 1 versions of the moves until you've built up the strength to take them on. When moves call for a resistance band, use a wider/heavier band than you used in Phase 1.

Weeks 1, 2, 5, 6   DAY 1

EXERCISE	SETS	REPS
1A) Forearm Front-Body Plank with Alternating Toe Lifts	2	30–60 seconds
1B) Side-Body Plank	2	30–60 seconds
2A) Pushup	3–4	6–8 (do higher reps for the eccentric version)
2B) Seated Resistance Band Row with a 10-second pause row on the last rep of each set	3–4	8–10
3A) Resistance Band Squat with a 10-second pause squat on the last rep of each set	3–4	10–12
3B) Walking Lunges	3–4	10–15 steps each leg
4) Slider Supine Hamstring Curl	3–4	10–12

DAY 2

EXERCISE	SETS	REPS
1A) Bear Crawl or Bear Hold	2	8–10 crawls forward then backward or 30 seconds
1B) Supine Hip Extension with Marching	2	10–12 with 10 reps of marching
2A) Resistance Band Squat to Overhead Press	3–4	8–10
2B) Resistance Band Deadlift	3–4	8–10
3) Resistance Band Good Morning	3–4	10–12
4A) Resistance Band Overhead Triceps Extension with a 10-second pulse hold on the last rep of each set	3–4	10–12 with pulse hold
4B) Resistance Band Biceps Curl with a 10-second pulse hold on the last rep of each set	3–4	10–12 with pulse hold

DAY 3

EXERCISE	SETS	REPS
1A) High Plank Shoulder Taps	2	8–10 each arm
1B) Supine Leg Lowers	2	10–12
2A) Resistance Band Squat to Chest Press	2–3	10–12
2B) Resistance Band Bent-Over Row	2–3	10–12
3A) Resistance Band Split Squat	2–3	10–12 each leg
3B) Frog Hip Thrust Pumps	2–3	20–30

(continued)

PHASE 2 ROUTINE (cont.)

Weeks 3, 4, 7, 8

DAY 1

EXERCISE	SETS	REPS
1A) Bear Crawl or Bear Hold	2	8 to 10 crawls forward then backward for 30 seconds
1B) Supine Hip Extension with Marching	2	10–12 with 10 reps of marching
2A) Resistance Band Squat to Overhead Press	3–4	8–10
2B) Resistance Band Deadlift	3–4	8–10
3A) Resistance Band Squat to Chest Press	2–3	10–12
3B) Resistance Band Bent-Over Row	2–3	10–12

DAY 2

EXERCISE	SETS	REPS
1A) High Plank Shoulder Taps	2	8–10 each arm
1B) Supine Leg Lowers	2	10–12
2A) Pushup	3–4	6–8 (do higher reps for the eccentric version)
2B) Seated Resistance Band Row with a 10-second pause row on the last rep of each set	3–4	8–10
3A) Resistance Band Split Squat	2–3	10–12 each leg
3B) Frog Hip Thrust Pumps	2–3	20–30

DAY 3

EXERCISE	SETS	REPS
1A) Forearm Front-Body Plank with Alternating Toe Lifts	2	30–60 seconds
1B) Side-Body Plank	2	30–60 seconds
2A) Resistance Band Overhead Triceps Extension with a 10-second pulse hold on the last rep of each set	3–4	10–12 with pulse hold
2B) Resistance Band Biceps Curl with a 10-second pulse hold on the last rep of each set	3–4	10–12 with pulse hold
3A) Walking Lunges	3–4	10–15 steps each leg
3B) Slider Supine Hamstring Curl	3–4	10–12

EXTRA CREDIT

Cap off your superset sessions with this calorie-crushing "finisher." Do each of the following exercises for 30 seconds with no rest in between. Then rest for 30 seconds after all four exercises have been completed in succession. Repeat two to four more times.

TRAVELING ZIGZAG SPEED SKATERS

Follow the Speed Skaters directions from Phase 1 (page 179), starting out on your right foot, but this time you will jump out to the side *and forward*, instead of just directly out to the side. Depending on how stable you feel, tap your left foot or keep it elevated once you land. You will do the same on the other foot until you have zigzagged two to three times forward and two to three times backward. Each time your foot makes contact with the ground is 1 rep.

BURPEES TO JUMP

Follow the Step Back, Stand Up Burpees directions in Phase 1 (page 180). For an extra challenge, jump up from your low squat position instead of standing back up.

HIGH PLANK OUTSIDE TOE TOUCHES

Get down into a high plank position with your arms slightly bent. Your body should form a straight line from your head to your ankles. Keeping your core tight, kick your right leg out to the side and reach for it with your right hand—touch your foot if you can! Then return your hand and foot to the starting position. That's 1 rep. Repeat on the other side.

AB BICYCLES
See directions for this move in Phase 1 (page 182).

CARDIO

In this phase, try more challenging, fat-torching cardio workouts like running, stairclimbing, jumping rope, or hilly outdoor road biking. Or do high-intensity interval training (HIIT) on the treadmill, bike, or elliptical: After a 5-minute warmup, go as hard as you can for 1 to 2 minutes, rest for at least the same amount of time, and then repeat this four to eight more times for a total of 15 to 30 minutes (starting at 15 and working up to 30). Or take advanced fitness classes (like boot camp or spinning) that have periods of intensity built into their programs. Here is an example.

Week 1

DAY 1	Go for a bike ride on hilly terrain for half an hour.
DAY 2	Take an advanced fitness class, like spinning, boot camp, or dance.
DAY 3	Do high-intensity interval training (HIIT) on the treadmill—After a 5-minute warmup, run as hard as you can for 1 to 2 minutes, rest for at least the same amount of time, and then repeat this four to eight more times for a total of 15 to 30 minutes (starting at 15 and working up to 30).

Week 2

DAY 1	Go for a 30-minute run at a pace that makes it difficult, if not impossible, to carry on a conversation.
DAY 2	Do HIIT on the elliptical. After a 5-minute warmup, go as hard as you can for 1 to 2 minutes, rest for at least the same amount of time, and then repeat this four to eight more times for a total of 15 to 30 minutes (starting at 15 and working up to 30).
DAY 3	Jump rope for 2 minutes, and then walk for 1 to 2 minutes to catch your breath; repeat this combination five times total for a 15- to 20-minute workout. (Since jumping rope is a very intense exercise, you can get away with 20 minutes instead of 30.)

Phase 3

*By now, you're probably getting close to Take It All Off!
The goal for the final 2 months is to refine and define your
physique by strength training four times a week, with each
session focusing on either upper body muscles or lower body
muscles. An ideal training schedule would be upper body on
Monday, lower body on Tuesday, cardio on Wednesday,
upper body on Thursday, cardio on Friday, and lower body
on Saturday, with Sunday as an "active rest" day. Your
strength workouts will last about 30 minutes, but to speed
up and enhance your results, cap off your strength routines
with 20 minutes of steady-state cardio. Warm up and stretch
just like you did in Phase 1 and Phase 2.*

STRENGTH TRAINING MOVES

Here are the new moves you'll need to complete Phase 3. You'll be breaking out the dumbbells for a few of these exercises, as certain moves lend themselves to hand weights instead of bands.

HOLLOW BODY HOLD

Lie flat on your back with your legs straight and arms overhead on the floor, palms up. Contract your abs and flatten your lower back to raise your arms, head, shoulders, and feet off the floor. Your body will form the shape of a banana. Hold this position for 10 to 30 seconds.

SIDEWAYS BEAR CRAWL

In a Bear Hold position (page 161) with your core tight and knees 1 to 2 inches off the ground, using your opposite arm and leg together to move, crawl to the right 8 to 10 times, and then switch directions and crawl to the left 8 to 10 times. Be sure to keep your knees off the ground the whole time—and don't let your body rock side to side as you crawl.

DUMBBELL CHEST FLY

Lie on your back with legs straight and feet flat on the floor. Bend knees to alleviate back pain. Grasp a light dumbbell (8 to 12 pounds) in each of your hands and raise and straighten your arms so they are perpendicular to the floor and above your chest. Keeping your abs tight, slowly lower the weights out to the sides of your body, opening your arms and keeping them straight. Stop when you feel a slight pull in your chest muscles. Contract your chest to bring the dumbbells back together, above your chest.

DUMBBELL BENT-OVER REAR DELT FLY

Stand tall with a light dumbbell in each hand. Bracing your abs, push your hips back to bend forward, keeping a slight bend in your knees. Your arms will be hanging below your body. Squeeze your shoulder blades together and pull to raise your arms up and out to the sides, keeping a slight bend to your elbows. Pause and then slowly lower the dumbbells back to the starting position.

DUMBBELL TRICEPS KICKBACK

Stand tall with a light dumbbell in your right hand. Bracing your abs, push your hips back to bend forward, keeping a slight bend in your knees. Rest your left hand on your left thigh or a chair or table. Bend your right arm 90 degrees. Squeeze your triceps to straighten your right arm out behind your body. Pause, squeezing your triceps, then slowly lower the weight back to the starting position. Repeat with your left arm.

PHASE 3 ROUTINE

Like Phase 2, Phase 3 includes supersets of exercises. If you see A and B after the exercise number, this means you will perform exercise A, immediately followed by exercise B, then rest for 1 minute and repeat for the desired amount of sets. If you are moving through these workouts at a fairly quick pace and stick with the lower set range, they should take you about 30 minutes. If you have more time and want more of a challenge, add in more sets, plus the 20 minutes of steady-state cardio (running, walking, biking, etc., at a steady pace).

DAY 1 UPPER BODY

EXERCISE	SETS	REPS
1A) Hollow Body Hold	2	10–30 seconds
1B) Sideways Bear Crawl	2	8–10 crawls to one side then the other
2A) Dumbbell Chest Fly	2–3	12–15
2B) Dumbbell Bent-Over Rear Delt Fly	2–3	12–15
3A) Pushup or Eccentric Pushup	3–4	As many reps as possible, with at least 6 reps
3B) Resistance Band Bent-Over Row	3–4	10–12
4A) Dumbbell Triceps Kickback	3–4	10–12 on each arm
4B) Resistance Band Biceps Curl	3–4	10–12

DAY 2 LOWER BODY

EXERCISE	SETS	REPS
1A) Bear Crawl or Bear Hold	2	8–10 crawls forward then backward or 30 seconds
1B) Supine Hip Extension with a 10-second hold at the top on the last rep of each set	2	10–12
2A) Resistance Band Squat with a 10-second pause squat on the last rep of each set	3–4	8–10
2B) Resistance Band Deadlift	3–4	8–10
3A) Resistance Band Good Morning	3–4	10–12
3B) Walking Lunges	3–4	10–12 steps each leg
4) Slider Supine Hamstring Curl or Feet Elevated Hip Extension (Phase 2)	3–4	10–12

DAY 3 UPPER BODY

EXERCISE	SETS	REPS
1A) High Plank Shoulder Taps	2	8–10 each arm
1B) Supine Leg Lowers	2	10–12
2A) Resistance Band Squat to Chest Press	2–3	12–15
2B) Seated Resistance Band Row	2–3	12–15
3A) Resistance Band Overhead Press	3–4	10–12
3B) Resistance Band Upright Row with Side Step	3–4	10–12 alternating sides
4A) Resistance Band Overhead Triceps Extension with a 10-second pulse hold on the last rep of each set	3–4	10–12 with pulse hold
4B) Resistance Band Biceps Curl with a 10-second pulse hold on the last rep of each set	3–4	10–12 with pulse hold

DAY 4 LOWER BODY

EXERCISE	SETS	REPS
1A) Sideways Bear Crawl	2	8–10 crawls to one side then the other
1B) Supine Hip Extension with Marching	2	10–12 with 10–12 marching steps
2A) Resistance Band Split Squat	3–4	10–12 each leg
2B) Resistance Band Deadlift	3–4	12–15
3A) Resistance Band Good Morning	3–4	12–15
3B) Frog Hip Thrust Pumps	2–3	20–30

CARDIO

To boost your calorie burn even more, you can add 20 minutes of steady-state cardio (at an intensity level of 6 to 8 out of 10) after each of your strength sessions. On nonstrength days, shoot for 15 to 30 minutes of HIIT using any of the cardio methods described in Phase 2. Here is an example.

Week 1

DAY 1	Do HIIT on the treadmill—After a 5-minute warmup, run as hard as you can for 1 to 2 minutes, rest for at least the same amount of time, and then repeat this four to eight more times for a total of 15 to 30 minutes (starting at 15 and working up to 30).
DAY 2	Do HIIT on a rowing machine. After a 5-minute warmup, row as hard as you can for 1 to 2 minutes, rest for at least the same amount of time, and then repeat this four to eight more times for a total of 15 to 30 minutes (starting at 15 and working up to 30).
DAY 3	Do a HIIT plyometric workout—1 minute of Jumping Jacks, followed by 1 minute of Speed Skaters, immediately followed by 1 minute of High Plank Jacks, followed by 1 minute of burpees (pick either option). Rest for 2 minutes and repeat this four more times.

Week 2

DAY 1	Do HIIT on a stationary bike. After a 5-minute warmup, pedal as hard as you can for 1 to 2 minutes, rest for at least the same amount of time, and then repeat this four to eight more times for a total of 15 to 30 minutes (starting at 15 and working up to 30).
DAY 2	Take a spin class at your local gym. Or go on a strenuous hike for at least 30 minutes.
DAY 3	Incorporate HIIT into an outdoor run while listening to music—Jog slowly for 5 minutes, run as hard as you can for one song, run slowly during the next song, and then repeat this four to eight more times for a total of 15 to 30 minutes (starting at 15 and working up to 30).

"I Did It!"

CHRISTINA'S STORY: As a high schooler, Christina didn't eat your standard bagged lunch. When she wasn't hitting the drive-thru with friends, she was chowing down on pizza from the restaurant her mother owned. "She would send the delivery guy to my school," says Christina. By the time she was 15, she stood 5 feet 7 inches and weighed 380 pounds.

NAME: **Christina Donatella**
AGE: **29**
HOMETOWN: **Barrie, Ontario**
BEFORE WEIGHT: **380**
AFTER WEIGHT: **200**

WAKE-UP CALL: Christina joined her high school choir on a trip to Italy. But a week in, she was forced to spend the day in bed while her classmates explored Rome. "I was too heavy and tired to move," she recalls. Humiliated, Christina resolved that she would never again let her weight limit what she could do.

SUCCESS SECRETS: Christina started doing her mom's old aerobics videos a few times a week and soon joined a gym to use the weight machines. She kissed the drive-thru goodbye and dropped 50 pounds in the next 7 months. Over 6 years, Christina whittled off 130 more pounds a little at a time by avoiding fast food and keeping up her gym habit. Later, Christina set up a Facebook page to get back on track and keep herself accountable. She posted photos of her progress and found an outpouring of support from the online community. "People I didn't even know started following along," she says. She reached an active and happy 200 pounds. Since then, she has become a certified personal trainer and took second place in a fitness show (transformation division) in Las Vegas. "I'm taken seriously now," says Christina. "I used to rely on being the funny, fat friend, but now people look up to me, and that's an honor."

10

Keeping It
All Off

If you're reading this chapter, chances are you've hit your weight loss goal—or are getting there—and are curious about what happens next. Congrats—either way—both take a mountain of courage! The good news is that if you've lost the weight, the blood, sweat, and tears stuff is over. Now that you're in shape, exercise (hopefully!) no longer feels like torture, and you've discovered workouts that are fun and rewarding. You've adopted healthy eating habits and developed a taste for nutritious foods like kale and quinoa. Now comes the second part of this plan, which is just as important as the first, and that's maintenance. See, the Take It All Off program doesn't help you lose weight and then leave you hanging; it establishes lifelong habits that will keep you at a healthy weight for good. In fact, 98 percent of our TIAO superstars, each profiled in the "You Lose, You Win" column of *Women's Health* magazine, have *kept the weight off* ever since!

A lot of people struggle to keep weight off after successfully slimming down.

Researchers at the National Institute of Diabetes and Digestive and Kidney Diseases were curious about why, so they tracked *The Biggest Loser* contestants from season eight for 6 years.[1] It turned out most of them gained back the weight they had fought so hard to lose. You might assume this occurred because the contestants no longer had Jillian and Bob counting their lunges and calories. But the researchers found it was more complicated than that.

The contestants' resting metabolic rates, the measure of calories burned during inactivity, had slowed down, so they weren't able to torch calories as effectively. Think of it like a fire burning within the body. A larger person has a big fire to burn calories. As that person loses weight—especially when she drops pounds quickly and drastically—the fire shrinks pretty dramatically. But the brain doesn't catch on that quickly—it still wants the person to seek out the same amount of food she ate when she weighed more.

The Take It All Off Plan is designed to help you lose a pound or two a week, and this reasonable pace gives the body a chance to readjust and reset at a natural rate. That's one of the ways this program is different from the diets and exercise regimes you might see featured on reality TV.

What's more, this program has armed you with the skills to stay at an optimal weight and handle any potential pitfalls. An analysis of data on weight loss maintenance, published in the *American Journal of Clinical Nutrition,*[2] identified six key strategies for keeping weight off—and they are all things you're already doing. They include engaging in high levels of physical activity (check), eating a diet low in calories and fat (check), eating breakfast (check), weighing yourself (check), maintaining a consistent eating pattern (check), and catching (and correcting) slipups fast (check). So it's a matter of sticking with your healthy new habits, especially for the next 2 to 5 years, when people are most at risk for packing it back on. (Research shows that after 2 to 5 years the chance of keeping it off forever significantly increases.[3])

Here are a few things you must do to keep the weight off.

Weigh yourself regularly. The research on weight maintenance favors daily weigh-ins, but stepping on the scale once a week is enough to keep you on track—and help you catch extra pounds creeping on before they turn into mega weight gain.

Exercise *at least* four times per week (or 225 to 300 minutes per week, which a review of research, published in *Progress in Cardiovascular Diseases,*[4] shows can prevent a normal-weight person from becoming overweight). Make sure at least 2 days are devoted to strength training, which will maintain muscle mass and keep your metabolism cranking. On other days, do cardio—ideally some HIIT workouts and some longer, steady-state routines—to burn calories.

"I Did It!"

ZAKIEE'S STORY: Fast-Food Heaven may not appear on any map, but it's how Zakiee refers to her Ohio hometown. Even before she became pregnant in 2005, the interior designer ate out or hit a drive-thru at least 4 nights a week—pushing her weight over 200 pounds. A year and a half after delivering a girl, Zakiee, who is 5 feet 6 inches, was still wearing a size 18. With a busy job and a new baby, "I didn't feel as if I had time to focus on myself," she says.

WAKE-UP CALL: Until her daughter was 18 months old, Zakiee believed her poor diet, low energy, and stubborn pregnancy pounds were just part of being a new mom. But as her daughter grew, Zakiee could no longer deny the truth. "I finally took a hard look at my health," she says.

SUCCESS SECRETS: After she discovered she was eating twice the recommended serving of most foods, Zakiee replaced fast food with healthy, low-cal recipes, such as whole wheat pasta loaded with veggies. Down to 187 pounds by June 2007, she learned she was pregnant again.

With her doctor's approval, she kept an eye on her portions, used the elliptical, walked, and did prenatal yoga three or four times a week until her son was born in February 2008. Weeks later, with her MD's permission, she was working out again. She added running, strength training, and kickboxing to her routine, and the number on the scale dropped to 134. "This is the least I've ever weighed as an adult!" she says. "I've completely transformed." Zakiee has kept the weight off.

NAME: **Zakiee Labib**
AGE: **35**
HOMETOWN: **Westlake, Ohio**
BEFORE WEIGHT: **238**
AFTER WEIGHT: **134**

Be conscious of calories. Recalculate your optimal daily calories based on your new weight (see the "Calorie Calculator" section on page 76), and aim to stay somewhere around that number each day. You don't need to make yourself crazy or do any official tallying; simply have a general idea of the caloric intake of each food you consume. After a while, you'll start to do this automatically.

Keep pumping up the protein. Take your new weight and multiply that number by 0.5 to find out how many grams of protein you need each day. Eat *at least* that amount (spread out over three meals and two snacks) to prevent hunger pangs and help build and repair muscle.

YOUR REAL-LIFE GAME PLAN

Diets have rules so you know exactly what to put in your mouth, and what to avoid. But postprogram life is full of unexpected obstacles and temptations. These strategies will help you navigate any situation.

Be a Creature of Habit

Eating the same things over and over may be boring, but it works like a charm. A review of research from the University at Buffalo[5] shows that dietary variety messes with our bodies' satiety cues and is associated with increased body weight. (Sampling lots of different flavors prevents us from feeling full, so we overeat.)

Another study from the *American Journal of Clinical Nutrition*[6] proved that eating the same flavor daily can help you consume less. Researchers gave a group of women a 28-minute task that helped them earn points. Each point was rewarded with a 125-calorie portion of mac and cheese. Half of the women repeated this experiment on 5 consecutive days, while the other half came in just once a week for 5 weeks. The once-a-day group starting reducing their intake of mac and cheese, while the once-a-weekers increased their intake. To wit: The everyday group got bored of mac and cheese pretty quickly, so they started eating less of it, while it continued to be a novelty to the once-a-week group, who gobbled it up. Having a rotation of snacks and meals that you know work for you minimizes the risk of overeating. Melanie Kitchen of Grand Island, New York, who lost 69 pounds, says having the same breakfast and lunch most days helped because she didn't have to come up with new recipes. That doesn't mean you shouldn't try new things once in while, but making most of your meals monotonous affords you the opportunity to savor new tastes a few times a week without any impact on your waistline.

Feel the Burn—Again

Monotony works for exercise, too. Sweating at the same time of day helps make exercise a ritual, something you do daily, automatically, and uncompromisingly, like brushing your teeth. Developing a passion for a form of exercise can improve consistency, as well. For example, Leanna Reilling runs; weight loss superstar Alexandra Shipper got into SoulCycle; Jen Punda is in a competitive volleyball league; Courtney Stearns boxes; sisters Jen Kelley and Kelly McCarthy are boot-camp junkies. The pull is even more powerful when you join forces with other exercisers who share your passion. Whether it's joining a running club or CrossFit box, playing on a sports team, or simply going to the same 9:00 a.m. workout class every day, with the same people and the same instructor, becoming part of a community of exercisers will keep you motivated (and help you make lifelong friends, too).

And while challenging your body with intense new workouts is associated with weight *loss*, doing the same type of routine over and over can be effective for weight *maintenance*. Basically, your body adjusts to whatever you're doing in an attempt to keep things status quo (bodies don't want to lose weight!). A new study published in the journal *Current Biology*[7] shows that the body adapts to increased exercise, meaning it stops burning extra calories when you work out more.

Experiment a Little

Finding your postdiet rhythm takes a little trial and error. You may be able to get away with eating more than you think you can, and because you've honed your willpower, you can trust yourself to make these small changes without slipping back into old patterns. If you want to start eating a small dessert every evening, try it for a few weeks. If the needle on the scale doesn't budge, great—you've proven that your diet and exercise habits can accommodate this daily indulgence. If the scale shows some weight gain, you'll just eat a smaller afternoon snack or exercise for an extra 15 minutes and see if that works for you.

What if you start gaining and you can't pinpoint it to a certain behavior, like eating that little dessert every night? Break out your food diary to find the flaws in your diet, and if you need to, go back to the Quick Start in Chapter 6 to reset your eating habits. Think of the Quick Start as a reboot, something you can do whenever you're feeling out of control or unhealthy. Or if your jeans are tighter than you'd like them to be.

Go Out without Gaining

Even people with healthy eating habits and extraordinary willpower tend to get tempted—and tripped up—when they're dining out or mingling at cocktail parties. Here are two secrets to special-occasion eating.

Look up the menu before you go. When you're busy catching up with friends or brokering a business deal over a meal, it can be easy to just order the first thing that looks appetizing. Or you make a rookie mistake like ordering the halibut without noticing it's breaded or prepared in a rich beurre blanc sauce. Scanning the menu ahead of time will save you time and calories. This tip helped Larissa Reggetto of Bethlehem, Pennsylvania, drop a whopping 105 pounds. "I look up restaurants' nutritional info online before I go out to eat so I can choose wisely," says Larissa.

Step away from the buffet. To avoid temptation and mindless eating, it's best to socialize away from where the food is stationed. A study out of the Cornell University Food and Brand Lab[8] found that people with higher BMIs were more likely to be seated at a table that offered a bird's-eye view of the food, as opposed to being seated facing away from the spareribs and fried rice.

Avoid the Two-App Trap

For a long time I would order two appetizers instead of one big meal, thinking it would help me eat less. Then I realized that my go-to app choices—tuna tartare (prepared with crème fraiche and avocado and surrounded by crostini) and pear and gorgonzola salad (which often comes topped with candied nuts)—packed more calories than many main dishes. So now I just try to have a main course, because the more courses you order, the more opportunities you have to overeat. If everyone else is ordering an app or I am simply too hungry to wait for my meal to come, I order a simple mixed green salad to start.

NAME: **JaLisa Maxwell**
AGE: **28**
HOMETOWN: **Tallahassee, Florida**
BEFORE WEIGHT: **205**
AFTER WEIGHT: **140**

Be a Politely Pushy Patron

I'm a little conflicted about this because I find it infuriating when people make all kinds of demands and substitutions at a restaurant.

But ultimately, you are paying for a meal so you deserve to have it prepared to your satisfaction. "Don't be scared to be picky; tell them what you want," says Florida native JaLisa Maxwell, who dropped 65 pounds.

Courteously ask the server to hold starchy sides—like mashed potatoes, pasta, or rice pilaf—and get extra veggies or mixed greens instead. Request your salad dressing on the side, or ask your server to hold the dressing and bring you olive oil and vinegar. Also ask your server to whisk away the breadbasket (as long as your dining partner doesn't mind—my usual dinner partner, my husband, does mind!). You get the picture. Do what you have to do to make your meal less filled with temptation.

Drink and Shrink!

The most encouraging piece of research I've come upon lately is that light to moderate alcohol intake may prevent you from gaining weight. The study, which was done at Brigham and Women's Hospital,[9] analyzed the boozing habits of almost 20,000 women over 13 years and found that those who drank one to two glasses of vino a day were less likely to pack on pounds than nondrinkers. (Women who drank red wine were the most successful at keeping off pounds.) It's a bit of a head scratcher, but one explanation is that women tend to eat less to make up for that glass (or two) of wine.

Keep in mind that one glass of wine is

4 ounces, and most of us pour ourselves double that. Buy smaller wine glasses, or invest in Wine-Trax, a wine and beverage glass that has frosted lines indicating how many servings you're pouring. Not a wine drinker? Other slimming sips include vodka soda (not Coke, but soda water), tequila over ice, or light beer.

INDULGE YOURSELF

To keep cravings at bay and avoid feelings of deprivation, allow yourself one small (under 150 calories) treat a day. One of my favorites is ricotta cheese—which has a hint of natural sweetness—dusted with cinnamon. Bridget Rauschenberg does something similar, but uses Greek yogurt instead of ricotta.

Caitlin Gallagher replaced her nightly bowl of ice cream with an apple or a square of dark chocolate. Brittany Hicks bakes mini versions of her favorite pies and cobblers, which gives her all the taste for a fraction of the fat, sugar, and calories. Katrina McCloud says, "I drink herbal tea after dinner to signal that dinner's over and to curb snacking."

Check out these yummy, tummy-flattening desserts that you can find in your local grocery or health food store.

VitaTops muffin top. This type of muffin top won't give you a muffin top. Each one of these palm-size baked goods contains 4 to 5 grams of protein, 4 to 9 grams of fiber, 1 to 3 grams of fat, and 100 to 120 calories. I am

NAME: **Caitlin Gallagher**
AGE: **42**
HOMETOWN: **Charlottesville, Virginia**
BEFORE WEIGHT: **290**
AFTER WEIGHT: **165**

Yasso Frozen Greek Yogurt bar. Glancing at the laundry list of artificial ingredients on the package of most low-cal ice cream bars is enough to make you lose your appetite (another diet trick I hadn't considered!). Yasso's bars are 150 calories max, pack 5 grams of protein, and are made with wholesome, recognizable ingredients. And most importantly, they are delicious—I should know, I eat one for dessert every night! My favorite flavors: chocolate chip, cookies 'n' cream, and cookie dough.

Homefree Vanilla Mini Cookies. When food companies take out gluten, they usually replace it with something even worse: sugar. Seven of these all-natural gluten-free cookies— which are also free of nuts, eggs, and milk— contain 10 grams of sugar and 150 calories, which is pretty impressive by cookie standards.

Emerald Cinnamon Roast Almonds 100-calorie pack. This portion-controlled bag of nuts has just enough cinnamon sweetness to count as a dessert. They contain a little artificial sweetener but are so good and otherwise healthy that I'm willing to let that slide.

Halo Top ice cream. Halo Top is so proud of the fact that an entire *pint* of its all-natural ice cream is only 280 calories that the company prints it on the front of the tub. Why hide this amazing info on the back? Per serving, the Vanilla Bean, Chocolate, Lemon Cake, and Mint Chip flavors of this frozen treat contain 60 calories, 6 grams of protein, 2 grams of fat, and only 4 grams of sugar. (Other flavors ring in at 70 calories per serving.)

obsessed with the Deep Chocolate flavor, which tastes like cake and is dotted with rich chocolate chips. These babies are completely preservative-free, which means you have to keep them in the freezer or they'll go bad.

"I Did It!"

NAME: **Sarah Russello**

AGE: **34**

HOMETOWN: **Clarks Summit, Pennsylvania**

BEFORE WEIGHT: **182**

AFTER WEIGHT: **135**

SARAH'S STORY: Sarah had vowed to stay at her college weight after taking a job as a sales rep. But she hit a snag when she met her future husband, Charles, in October 2008. Her gym workouts fell by the wayside as she spent more time with Charles, a martial-arts master who could easily burn off the calories from their dinners out. Sarah, who matched him bite for bite, wasn't so lucky. By March 2010, she carried 40 extra pounds on her 5-foot-7-inch frame.

WAKE-UP CALL: A friend tagged Sarah in a Facebook photo. Sarah was sitting at a bar in front of a huge plate of mozzarella sticks, beer in one hand, cigarette in the other, with her extra pounds hanging over her jeans. "I didn't recognize myself," she says. She knew she had to get her body back.

SUCCESS SECRETS: Sarah tackled her three-packs-a-week habit first. "I thought, 'Why bother trying to lose weight if I'll just gain it back when I stop smoking?'" she says. Within a few weeks, she'd swapped the smokes for gum. "Quitting smoking made me feel like if I could do that, I could do anything," she says. Sarah scaled back her portion sizes and swapped sweet tea for water. In June 2010, Sarah returned to the gym, where she alternated between strength training and cardio days. The following June, when Sarah married Charles, the size-8 gown she'd ordered had to be taken in.

Sarah has kept her weight at 135 despite a slew of setbacks. The day after she returned from maternity leave with her son, Sarah was let go from her job. Then Charles was diagnosed with cancer, and then her mom passed away unexpectedly. After months of treatment, Charles was declared cancer-free. The experience gave Sarah a new perspective on life and health. "Think about your 'why,'" Sarah says. "My 'why' is my family. I don't want to end up like my mom, who passed away unhealthy at a young age. I want to be there for my family."

Endnotes

Chapter 1

1   N. Lasikiewicz, K. Myrissa, A. Hoyland, and C. L. Lawton, "Psychological Benefits of Weight Loss following Behavioural and/or Dietary Weight Loss Interventions. A Systematic Research Review," *Appetite* 72 (2013): 123–37.

2   I. J. Perron, A. I. Pack, and S. Veasey, "Diet/Energy Balance Affect Sleep and Wakefulness Independent of Body Weight," *SLEEP* 38, no. 12 (2015): 1893–903.

3   T. Byers and R. L. Sedjo, "Does Intentional Weight Loss Reduce Cancer Risk?," *Diabetes, Obesity and Metabolism* 13, no. 12 (2011): 1063–72.

4   R. F. Hamman, R. R. Wing, S. L. Edelstein, et al., "Effect of Weight Loss with Lifestyle Intervention on Risk of Diabetes," *Diabetes Care* 29, no. 9 (2006): 2102–7.

5   R. S. Legro, W. C. Dodson, P. M. Kris-Etherton, et al., "Randomized Controlled Trial of Preconception Interventions in Infertile Women with Polycystic Ovary Syndrome," *Journal of Clinical Endocrinology & Metabolism* 100, no. 11 (2015): 4048–58.

6   F. Magkos, G. Fraterrigo, J. Yoshino, et al., "Effects of Moderate and Subsequent Progressive Weight Loss on Metabolic Function and Adipose Tissue Biology in Humans with Obesity," *Cell Metabolism* 23, no. 4 (2016): 591–601.

7   J. E. Neter, B. E. Stam, F. J. Kok, D. E. Grobbee, and J. M. Geleijnse, "Influence of Weight Reduction on Blood Pressure: A Meta-Analysis of Randomized Controlled Trials," *Hypertension* 42, no. 5 (2003) 878–84.

8   K. Johansson, J. Sundström, C. Marcus, E. Hemmingsson, and M. Neovius, "Risk of Symptomatic Gallstones and Cholecystectomy after a Very-Low-Calorie Diet or Low-Calorie Diet in a Commercial Weight Loss Program: 1-Year Matched Cohort Study," *International Journal of Obesity* 38, no. 2 (2014): 279–84.

9   S. P. Messier, D. J. Gutekunst, C. Davis, and P. DeVita, "Weight Loss Reduces Knee-Joint Loads in Overweight and Obese Older Adults with Knee Osteoarthritis," *Arthritis & Rheumatism* 52, no. 7 (2005): 2026–32.

10 R. L. Kolotkin, M. Binks, R. D. Crosby, T. Østbye, J. E. Mitchell, and G. Hartley, "Improvements in Sexual Quality of Life after Moderate Weight Loss," *International Journal of Impotence Research* 20, no. 5 (2008): 487–92.

11 R. S. Ahima and M. A. Lazar, "The Health Risk of Obesity—Better Metrics Imperative," *Science* 341, no. 6148 (2013): 856–58.

Chapter 2

1   P. Lally, C. H. M. van Jaarsveld, H. W. W. Potts, and J. Wardle, "How Are Habits Formed: Modelling Habit Formation in the Real World," *European Journal of Social Psychology* 40, no. 6 (2010): 998–1009.

2   B. Wansink, A. S. Hanks, and K. Kaipainen, "Slim by Design: Kitchen Counter Correlates of Obesity," *Health Education & Behavior* 43, no. 5 (2016): 552–58.

3   L. R. Vartanian, K. M. Kernan, and B. Wansink, "Clutter, Chaos, and Overconsumption: The Role of Mind-Set in Stressful and Chaotic Food Environments," *Environment & Behavior* (February 2, 2016): doi:10.1177/0013916516628178.

4   C. J. Courtemanche, J. C. Pinkston, C. J. Ruhm, and G. Wehby, "Can Changing Economic Factors Explain the Rise in Obesity?," *Southern Economic Journal* 82, no. 4 (2016): 1266–310.

5   J. F. Hollis, C. M. Gullion, V. J. Stevens, et al., "Weight Loss during the Intensive Intervention Phase of the Weight-Loss Maintenance Trial," *American Journal of Preventive Medicine* 35, no. 2 (2008): 118–26.

6   Y. Zheng, L. E. Burke, C. A. Danford, L. J. Ewing, M. A. Terry, and S. M. Sereika, "Patterns of Self-Weighing Behavior and Weight Change in a Weight Loss Trial," *International Journal of Obesity* 40, no. 9 (2016): 1392–96.

7   C. R. Pacanowski and D. A. Levitsky, "Frequent Self-Weighing and Visual Feedback for Weight Loss in Overweight Adults," *Journal of Obesity* 2015 (May 12, 2015): doi:10.1155/2015/763680.

8   M. Shimizu, K. Johnson, and B. Wansink, "In Good Company. The Effect of an Eating Companion's Appearance on Food Intake," *Appetite* 83 (December 2014): 263–68.

9   "Motivational Losing: Being the Weak Link in Team Activities May Lead to Longer, More Intense Workouts," Kansas State University, November 26, 2012, k-state.edu/today/announcement.php?id=6096.

10 A.N. Vgontzas, S. Pejovic, E. Zoumakis, et al., "Daytime Napping after a Night of Sleep Loss Decreases Sleepiness, Improves Performance, and Causes Beneficial Changes in Cortisol and Interleukin-6 Secretion," *American Journal of Physiology—Endocrinology and Metabolism* 292, no. 1 (2007): 253–61.

Chapter 3

1   B. Wansink, K. van Ittersum, and J. E. Painter, "Ice Cream Illusions: Bowls, Spoons, and Self-Served Portion Sizes," *American Journal of Preventive Medicine* 31, no. 3 (2006): 240–43.

2   J. A. Wolfson and S. N. Bleich, "Is Cooking at Home Associated with Better Diet Quality or Weight-Loss Intention?" *Public Health Nutrition* 18, no. 8 (2015): 1397–406.

3   L. E. Urban, J. L. Weber, M. B. Heyman, et al., "Energy Contents of Frequently Ordered Restaurant Meals and Comparison with Human Energy Requirements and US Department of Agriculture Database Information: A Multisite Randomized Study," *Journal of the Academy of Nutrition and Dietetics* 116, no. 4 (2016): 590–98.

4   W. Mischel, *The Marshmallow Test: Mastering Self-Control* (Boston: Little, Brown and Company, 2014).

5   T. O. Daniel, C. M. Stanton, L. H. Epstein, "The Future Is Now: Comparing the Effect of Episodic Future Thinking on Impulsivity in Lean and Obese Individuals," *Appetite*, vol. 71 (2013) 120–25.

6   L. R. Vartanian, W. H. Chen, N. M. Reily, and A. D. Castel, "The Parallel Impact of Episodic Memory and Episodic Future Thinking on Food Intake," *Appetite* 101 (June 2016): 31–36.

7   D. D. Wagner, M. Altman, R. G. Boswell, W. M. Kelley, and T. F. Heatherton, "Self-Regulatory Depletion Enhances Neural Responses to Rewards and Impairs Top-Down Control," *Psychological Science* 24, no. 11 (2013): 2262–71.

8   J. P. Redden and K. L. Haws, "Healthy Satiation: The Role of Decreasing Desire in Effective Self-Control," *Journal of Consumer Research* 39, no. 5 (2013): 1100–14.

Chapter 4

1   A. R. Skov, S. Toubro, B. Rønn, L. Holm, and A. Astrup, "Randomized Trial on Protein vs Carbohydrate in Ad Libitum Fat Reduced Diet for the Treatment of Obesity," *International Journal of Obesity* 23, no. 5 (1999): 528–36.

2   Ibid.

3   A. Pan, Q. Sun, A. M. Bernstein, et al., "Red Meat Consumption and Mortality: Results from Two Prospective Cohort Studies," *Archives of Internal Medicine* 172, no. 7 (2012): 555–63.

4   Y. Ma, B. C. Olendzki, J. Wang, et al., "Single-Component versus Multicomponent Dietary Goals for the Metabolic Syndrome: A Randomized Trial," *Annals of Internal Medicine* 162, no. 4 (2015): 248–57.

5   A. E. Mesas, M. Muñoz-Pareja, E. López-García, and F. Rodríguez-Artalejo, "Selected Eating Behaviours and Excess Body Weight: A Systematic Review," *Obesity Reviews* 13, no. 2 (2012): 106–35.

6   D. G. Schlundt, J. O. Hill, T. Sbrocco, J. Pope-Cordle, and T. Sharp, "The Role of Breakfast in the Treatment of Obesity: A Randomized Clinical Trial," *American Journal of Clinical Nutrition* 55, no. 3 (1992): 645–51.

7   A. Geliebter, N. M. Astbury, R. Aviram-Friedman, E. Yahav, and S. Hashim, "Skipping Breakfast Leads to Weight Loss but Also Elevated Cholesterol Compared with Consuming Daily Breakfasts of Oat Porridge or Frosted Cornflakes in Overweight Individuals: A Randomised Controlled Trial," *Journal of Nutritional Science* 3 (November 13, 2014): doi:10.1017/jns.2014.51.

8   J. D. Cameron, M. J. Cyr, and E. Doucet, "Increased Meal Frequency Does Not Promote Greater Weight Loss in Subjects Who Were Prescribed an 8-Week Equi-Energetic Energy-Restricted Diet," *British Journal of Nutrition* 103, no. 8 (2010): 1098–101.

9   M. Pomerleau, P. Imbeault, T. Parker, and E. Doucet, "Effects of Exercise Intensity on Food Intake and Appetite in Women," *American Journal of Clinical Nutrition* 80, no. 5 (2004): 1230–36.

10 H. Kahleova, L. Belinova, H. Malinska, et al. "Eating Two Larger Meals a Day (Breakfast and Lunch) Is More Effective Than Six Smaller Meals in a Reduced-Energy Regimen for Patients with Type 2 Diabetes: A Randomised Crossover Study," *Diabetologia* 57, no. 8 (2014): 1552–60.

11 S. E. Swithers, "Artificial Sweeteners Produce the Counterintuitive Effect of Inducing Metabolic Derangements," *Trends in Endocrinology & Metabolism* 24, no. 9 (2013): 431–41.

12 R. An, "Beverage Consumption in Relation to Discretionary Food Intake and Diet Quality among US Adults, 2003 to 2012," *Journal of the Academy of Nutrition and Dietetics* 116, no. 1 (2016): 28–37.

13 T. Tylka, R. M. Calogero, and S. Daníelsdóttir, "Is Intuitive Eating the Same as Flexible Dietary Control? Their Links to Each Other and Well-Being Could Provide an Answer," *Appetite* 95 (December 2015): 166–75.

14 M. Shah, J. Copeland, L. Dart, B. Adams-Huet, A. James, and D. Rhea, "Slower Eating Speed Lowers Energy Intake in Normal-Weight but Not Overweight/Obese Subjects," *Journal of the Academy of Nutrition and Dietetics* 114, no. 3 (2104): 393–402.

15 J. Ogden, E. Oikonomou, and G. Alemany, "Distraction, Restrained Eating and Disinhibition: An Experimental Study of Food Intake and the Impact of 'Eating on the Go,'" *Journal of Health Psychology* (August 2015): doi:10.1177/1359105315595119.

Chapter 5

1   A. Lehri and R. Mokha, "Effectiveness of Aerobic and Strength Training in Causing Weight Loss and Favourable Body Composition in Females," *Journal of Exercise Science and Physiotherapy* 2 (2006): 96–99.

2   S. H. Boutcher, "High-Intensity Intermittent Exercise and Fat Loss," *Journal of Obesity* 2011 (2011): doi:10.1155/2011/868305.

3   A. P. Wroblewski, F. Amati, M. A. Smiley, B. Goodpaster, and V. Wright, "Chronic Exercise Preserves Lean Muscle Mass in Masters Athletes," *Physician and Sportsmedicine* 39, no. 3 (2011): 172–78.

4   F. B. Willis, F. M. Smith, and A. P. Willis, "Frequency of Exercise for Body Fat Loss: A Controlled, Cohort Study," *Journal of Strength and Conditioning Research* 23, no. 8 (2009): 2377–80.

Chapter 6

1   T. S. Conner, K. L. Brookie, A. C. Richardson, and M. A. Polak, "On Carrots and Curiosity: Eating Fruit and Vegetables Is Associated with Greater Flourishing in Daily Life," *British Journal of Health Psychology* 20, no. 2 (2015): 413–27.

2   C. X. Muñoz, E. C. Johnson, A. L. McKenzie, et al. "Habitual Total Water Intake and Dimensions of Mood in Healthy Young Women," *Appetite* 92 (September 2015): 81–86.

Chapter 7

1   L. E. Armstrong, A. C. Pumerantz, M. W. Roti, et al., "Fluid, Electrolyte and Renal Indices of Hydration during 11 Days of Controlled Caffeine Consumption," *International Journal of Sport Nutrition and Exercise Metabolism* 15, no. 3 (2005): 252–65.

2   M. B. Zemel, J. Richards, S. Mathis, A. Milstead, L. Gebhardt, and E. Silva, "Dairy Augmentation of Total and Central Fat Loss in Obese Subjects," *International Journal of Obesity* 29, no. 4 (2005): 391–97.

3   J. S. Vander Wal, A. Gupta, P. Khosla, and N. V. Dhurandhar, "Egg Breakfast Enhances Weight Loss," *International Journal of Obesity* 32, no. 10 (2008): 1545–51.

4   N. M. McKeown, L. M. Troy, P. F. Jacques, U. Hoffmann, C. J. O'Donnell, and C. S. Fox, "Whole- and Refined-Grain Intakes Are Differentially Associated with Abdominal Visceral and Subcutaneous Adiposity in Healthy Adults: The Framingham Heart Study," *American Journal of Clinical Nutrition* 92, no. 5 (2010): 1165–71.

5   H. Poudyal, S. K. Panchal, J. Waanders, L. Ward, and L. Brown, "Lipid Redistribution by α-Linolenic Acid-Rich Chia Seed Inhibits Stearoyl-CoA Desaturase-1 and Induces Cardiac and Hepatic Protection in Diet-Induced Obese Rats," *Journal of Nutritional Biochemistry* 23, no. 2 (2012): 153–62.

6   L. Di Renzo, M. Rizzo, F. Sarlo, et al. "Effects of Dark Chocolate in a Population of Normal Weight Obese Women: A Pilot Study," *European Review for Medical and Pharmacological Sciences* 17, no. 16 (2012): 2257–66.

Chapter 8

1   S. Whiting, E. Derbyshire, and B. K. Tiwari, "Capsaicinoids and Capsinoids. A Potential Role for Weight Management? A Systematic Review of the Evidence," *Appetite* 59, no. 2 (2012): 341–48.

2   I. A. Sobenin, L. V. Nedosugova, L. V. Filatova, M. I. Balabolkin, T. V. Gorchakova, and A. N. Orekhov, "Metabolic Effects of Time-Released Garlic Powder Tablets in Type 2 Diabetes Mellitus: The Results of Double-Blinded Placebo-Controlled Study," *Acta Diabetologica* 45, no. 1 (2008): 1–6.

3   K. H. Han, C. H. Lee, M. Kinoshita, C. H. Oh, K. Shimada, and M. Fukushima, "Spent Turmeric Reduces Fat Mass in Rats Fed a High-Fat Diet," *Food & Function* 7, no. 4 (2016): 1814–24.

4   A. Magistrelli and J. C. Chezem, "Effect of Ground Cinnamon on Postprandial Blood Glucose Concentration in Normal-Weight and Obese Adults," *Journal of the Academy of Nutrition and Dietetics* 112, no. 11 (2012): 1806–9.

5   M. L. Assunção, H. S. Ferreira, A. F. dos Santos, C. R. Cabral CR Jr., and T. M. Florêncio, "Effects of Dietary Coconut Oil on the Biochemical and Anthropometric Profiles of Women Presenting Abdominal Obesity," *Lipids* 44, no. 7 (2009): 593–601.

6   D. Sankar, M. Ramakrishna Rao, G. Sambandam, and K. V. Pugalendid, "Effect of Sesame Oil on Diuretics or ß-blockers in the Modulation of Blood Pressure, Anthropometry, Lipid Profile, and Redox Status," *Yale Journal of Biology and Medicine* 70, no.1 (2007): 19–26.

Chapter 10

1   E. Fothergill, J. Guo, L. Howard, et al., "Persistent Metabolic Adaptation 6 Years after 'The Biggest Loser' Competition," *Obesity* 24, no. 8 (2016): 1612–19.

2   R. R. Wing and S. Phelan, "Long-Term Weight Loss Maintenance," *American Journal of Clinical Nutrition* 82, no. 1 (2005): 2225–55.

3   Ibid.

4   D. Swift, N. M. Johannsen, C. J. Lavie, C. P. Earnest, and T. S. Church, "The Role of Exercise and Physical Activity in Weight Loss and Maintenance," *Progress in Cardiovascular Diseases* 56, no. 4 (2014): 441–47.

5   H. A. Raynor and L. H. Epstein, "Dietary Variety, Energy Regulation, and Obesity," *Psychological Bulletin* 127, no. 3 (2001): 325–41.

6   L. H. Epstein, K. A. Carr, M. D. Cavanaugh, R. A. Paluch, and M. E. Bouton, "Long-Term Habituation to Food in Obese and Nonobese Women," *American Journal of Clinical Nutrition* 94, no. 2 (2011): 371–76.

7   H. Pontzer, R. Durazo-Arvizu, L. R. Dugas, et al. "Constrained Total Energy Expenditure and Metabolic Adaptation to Physical Activity in Adult Humans," *Current Biology* 26, no. 3 (2016): 410–17.

8   B. Wansink and C. R. Payne, "Eating Behavior and Obesity at Chinese Restaurants," *Obesity* 16, no. 8 (2008): 1957–60.

9   L. Wang, I. M. Lee, J. E. Manson, J. E. Buring, and H. D. Sesso, "Alcohol Consumption, Weight Gain, and Risk of Becoming Overweight in Middle-Aged and Older Women," *JAMA Internal Medicine* 170, no. 5 (2010): 453–61.

Photo Credits

Mitch Mandel: all exercise photos

Kenny Braun: cover and pages vi, vii, 15, 175

Andrew Cebulka: cover and pages vii, 34

Anthony Cunanan: cover

Ryan Donnell: cover and pages vii, 227

Matt Eich: cover and pages vii, 226

Joe Jaszewski: cover and page 4

Ray McCrea Jones: cover and page vi, 43

Roger Kisby: cover

Jamie Kripke: cover and pages vi, 53

Jared Leeds: page 105

John Loomis: cover and pages vii, 224

Ryan Lowry: cover and pages vii, 28

Matthew Mahon: cover and pages vii, 65

Ross Mantle: cover and pages vi, vii, 70

Robbie McClaran: cover and pages vii, 60

Erik Ostling: cover and pages vii, 46

Nathan Ellis Perkel: cover and pages vi, 56

Mark Peterman: cover and pages vi, 17

Nick Pironio: cover and pages vi, vii, 7

George Qua-Enoo: cover and pages vii, 217

Matt Rainey: cover and pages vii, 59

Greg Ruffing: cover and pages vi, vii, 22, 25, 62, 221

Kenneth Ruggiano: cover and pages 31

Jeffery Salter: cover and pages vi, vii, p. 3, 73

Ben Sklar: cover and pages vii, 80

Tim Soter: cover and pages vi

Jonathan Sprague: cover and page 9

Ben Stechschulte: cover and pages vii, 48

Kevin Steele: cover and pages vi, 33

Jason Wallis: cover and pages vi, 140

Index

Underscored page references indicate sidebars. **Boldface** references indicate photographs and illustrations.